Sheltering the Fugitive?

The Extradition of Irish Political Offenders

MICHAEL FARRELL

THE MERCIER PRESS
Cork and Dublin

The Mercier Press Limited
4 Bridge Street, Cork
24 Lower Abbey Street, Dublin 1

British Library Cataloguing in Publication Data

Farrell, Michael, 1944-

Sheltering the Fugitive?

1. Extradition—Political aspects—Ireland

2. Extradition—Political aspects—Great Britain

I. Title

341.4'88   KDK1800

ISBN 0-85342-750-X

Printed by Litho Press Co., Midleton, Co. Cork.

Contents

1: 'Violating the Rules of Hospitality'

'You have violated the rules of hospitality. Such a thing has not happened among the most barbarous hordes of the desert,' Napoleon Bonaparte, First Consul of France, wrote to the city of Hamburg on 30 December 1799. He was protesting at the city's decision to extradite the Dublin United Irishman James Napper Tandy and three companions to Britain.[1]

'Your fellow citizens will blame you forever for this,' Napoleon went on. 'The unfortunates whom you have handed over will die illustrious, but their blood will do more harm to their persecutors than any army could have done.'

Controversy over the extradition of Irish rebels is nothing new. The Napper Tandy case caused a political crisis in Europe at the time and held up the signing of a peace treaty between France and England.

Napper Tandy was one of the United Irish leaders who fled to revolutionary France, then at war with England, and sought French aid for the 1798 rebellion. He set out for Ireland by ship in September 1798 with supplies for General Humbert's French army at Killala but arrived in Donegal only to find that Humbert had been defeated and the rebellion was over.

Tandy tried to return to France but was forced to land in Norway and to try to make his way to Paris via the neutral city-state of Hamburg. He and three companions were arrested in Hamburg in November 1798 and the British ambassador demanded their extradition. France protested that Tandy was a general in the French army and demanded their release. The Hamburg authorities dithered. They were more sympathetic to Britain, but whatever they did it would lead to trouble.

The British threatened them and the Czar of Russia took a hand. He cut off all trade with Hamburg until Tandy was extradited and all revolutionary clubs in the city closed down. In September 1799 the four Irishmen were handed over to Britain. The French were furious. They broke off diplomatic and trading relations with Hamburg and when the city government tried to explain themselves, Napoleon wrote his angry letter. Eventually the Hamburg authorities apologised publicly and in 1801 they paid France a fine of four and a half million francs.

Tandy and his companions were tried in Ireland for their part in the rebellion. The others were treated leniently, but Tandy was sentenced to death at Lifford court in May 1801. The Hamburg government had pressed the British not to execute him and he was reprieved and ordered to be transported to Australia.

By then the war was going well for France and the British were suing for peace. France insisted on Tandy's release before the signing of the Treaty of Amiens and on 14 March 1802 he arrived in Bordeaux where he was given a civic reception and a military pension. He died eighteen months later.

Tandy was by no means the first Irish political refugee to seek refuge from the British authorities in other countries. Before him the most famous fugitives had been Hugh O'Neill, Earl of Tyrone and Rory O'Donnell, Earl of Tyrconnell, who fled to Spain in 1607, afraid they were about to be arrested and charged with treason. They and their entourage of lesser Ulster chieftains were welcomed at the court of Spain, England's traditional enemy.

After the Williamite wars at the end of the seventeenth century many Irish soldiers from the defeated Jacobite armies sought refuge on the continent and one of the earliest recorded extradition cases in modern times was when the

Estates General of Holland voted in October 1695 to hand over an Irish Jacobite fugitive to England — ruled by the Dutchman William III. The Irishman had hijacked a merchant ship sailing from Holland to England and had tried to divert it to Norway.

There was very little law on extradition before the eighteenth century. Before that governments did not care what happened to ordinary criminals if they left their territory. They were much more concerned about political offenders, rebels or rival claimants to the throne. But whether political fugitives were handed over by one state to another depended on the whim and the political calculation of the host country. Hostile powers usually gave refuge to each other's fugitives.

During the eighteenth century the growth of European trade and commerce made fugitive common criminals more of a problem and neighbouring states and trading partners began to make extradition agreements. But democratic and revolutionary ideas were spreading too and after the American and French revolutions the new republics became havens for political fugitives from many countries, notably Ireland. Theobald Wolfe Tone went to the United States in 1796 and then to France.

The new French constitution of 1793 declared that the republic would give asylum to foreigners banished from their own countries because of their love of freedom, but would refuse shelter to tyrants. Napoleon became less concerned for political refugees as he became more despotic at home but the idea of protecting fugitives spread in the more democratic states of Western Europe. Belgium passed the first formal extradition law in 1833, empowering the government to make extradition treaties with other states but forbidding the extradition of anyone wanted for a 'political offence' or for an offence 'connected to such an offence'.

The reasoning behind the growing acceptance of this 'political offence exception' to extradition was a mixture of idealism and pragmatism. Public opinion in the more democratic states had rejected the idea of the divine right of kings and accepted that it was legitimate to struggle against an oppressive government. There was also concern that alleged political offenders would not get a fair trial from the regimes they had tried to overthrow.

On the more pragmatic level it was argued that political offences were not crimes against the overall international public order. Unlike thieves, for example, who could be expected to ply their trade wherever they found themselves, political fugitives would not usually seek to overthrow the government of the country in which they had sought refuge. And, of course, there was the supremely pragmatic argument, which was to be so strikingly borne out in the twentieth century, that this year's rebels might well turn out to be next year's rulers and it would be foolish to commit yourself too firmly to one side or the other in a given conflict.

France, the United States and Britain had also accepted the 'political exception', though it was not spelled out in Britain until 1852 when the London government signed an extradition treaty with Belgium which included the political exception clause. By then a series of liberal or nationalist uprisings had swept Europe in 1848 only to be crushed within a few years and a stream of political refugees had reached Britain, which had begun to pride itself on offering a refuge to exiles from repressive regimes. The most famous political refugee of all, Karl Marx, arrived in London in 1849 and spent the rest of his life there, plotting the overthrow of the capitalist system.

Lord Palmerston, the British Foreign Secretary and later Prime Minister, stoutly defended the refusal of Britain and its ally Turkey to hand over the 1848 revolutionaries to the regimes they had opposed. 'The laws of hospitality,' he said, 'the dictates of humanity, the general feeling of mankind, forbid such surrender and any independent government which of its own free will were to make such surrender would be deservedly and universally stigmatised and dishonoured.'

There had of course been a rising in Ireland as well in 1848. British liberalism did not stretch as far as offering an amnesty to the defeated rebels and they sought refuge in France (James Stephens and John O'Mahony) and the United States (John Mitchel and Thomas Francis Meagher). The tradition of harbouring political refugees was so well established by then that the British made no real effort to have them sent back. They were to be followed by many more Irish fugitives right up to the present day. Indeed by 1922 the Irish revolutionary movement owed a considerable debt to those countries which had offered shelter to the Fenians and to members of the IRB and later the IRA on the run from the British authorities.

Eventually, in 1866, the British parliament discussed its first Extradition Bill. It did not clearly safeguard political offenders and the British philosopher John Stuart Mill and a number of other Independent Liberal MPs combined to defeat it. A new Bill which was passed in 1870 spelled out the political exception unambiguously. Mill commented in his autobiography: 'The cause of European freedom (was) thus . . . saved from a serious misfortune, and our country from a great iniquity.'

The 1870 Act was to form the basis of Irish extradition law as well until 1965. Under it fugitive offenders were to be handed over to other countries with which extradition treaties had been concluded, but 'no person is to be surrendered if his offence is one of a political character, or if he proves . . . that the requisition for his surrender has in fact been made with a view to try to punish him for an offence of a political character.'

The Act laid down the procedure for extradition hearings. The requesting country must notify the British authorities who would get a magistrate to issue a warrant for the suspect. Extradition would be granted only for fairly serious offences which corresponded to offences under British law. Once arrested the suspect would be brought before a magistrate's court. The requesting country would have to show that there was a *prima facie* case against the accused. Then, if all appeared to be in order, the magistrate would order the extradition.

If the fugitive wished to challenge the order either on technical grounds or by claiming that the offence was 'of a political character', he/she would have fifteen days in which to apply to the High Court for a writ of *habeas corpus* and the court could quash the order.

Over the next twenty years Britain signed extradition treaties with many countries and they all contained the political offence exception, but there was no attempt to define the phrase 'offence . . . of a political character' until the Castioni case in 1891.

Angelo Castioni was a sculptor and marble cutter from the canton of Ticino in Switzerland. He was an opponent of the Conservative local government in Ticino and had lived in London for seventeen years.

In 1890 trouble flared up in Ticino. The Liberal and Radical parties demanded a referendum to change the electoral laws which they claimed were loaded against them. The canton government refused and on 11 September 1890 an angry crowd raided the municipal armoury in Bellinzona, the chief town of the canton, seized some weapons and attacked the headquarters of the canton government.

Castioni had been in Italy buying marble and was passing through Bellinzona when the trouble came to a head. He took a leading part in the uprising and during the attack on the government building, he shot dead Luigi Rossi, a member of the Conservative administration. The crowd occupied the government building, imprisoned the Conservatives and set up a Liberal provisional government.

A few days later the federal government sent troops to Ticino and deposed the provisional government, but a referendum was eventually held and by 1892 Ticino had the most democratic constitution in Switzerland. In the meantime Castioni had fled back to London and the Swiss government sought his extradition on a charge of murder.

Castioni pleaded that the killing of Rossi was 'an offence of a political character' and so exempt from extradition. The case was heard in London by the Queen's Bench division of the English High Court. Castioni was represented by Sir Charles Russell QC, the distinguished Irish-born lawyer and Liberal MP who later became Lord Chief Justice of England as Lord Russell of Killowen.

Russell quoted two definitions of a political offence. One was by John Stuart Mill, who said in the House of Commons in 1867 that 'any offence committed in the course of, or furthering of, civil war, insurrection or commotion is a political offence.' The second definition was from Justice Sir James Fitzjames Stephens' *History of the Criminal Law of England*. Stephens was one of the three judges hearing the case.

Stephens had said: 'I think therefore that the expression "offence of a political character" . . . ought . . . to be interpreted to mean that fugitive criminals are not to be surrendered for extradition crimes if those crimes were incidental to and formed part of political disturbances.' Russell argued that under either definition Castioni's offence was political.

Castioni's extradition was refused. The judgement in the case was to become the classic text of extradition law on the question of the political exception and has been quoted in every major case since then.[2]

Justice Denham rejected John Stuart Mill's definition as too wide-reaching; it took no account of the object or intention of the actor. He did not think it necessary or desirable to give an exhaustive definition of a political offence, but said: 'To exclude extradition for such an act as murder . . . it must at least be shown that the act is done in furtherance of, done with the intention of assistance, as a sort of overt act in the course of acting in a political matter, a political uprising, or a dispute between two parties in the state as to which is to have the government in its hands . . . .'

He examined Castioni's offence to see if it satisfied these criteria, noting that 'there was more than a mere small rising of a few people against the law of the state . . . . There was something of a very serious character going on — amounting . . . in that small community, to a state of war.' The Swiss government itself regarded it as 'a serious political uprising' and Castioni had been 'an active party in the movement'.

It was not the court's business to decide whether the killing of Rossi was 'a wise act to promote the cause' or was necessary for its success. 'The question really is, whether, upon the facts, it is clear that the man was acting as one of a number of persons engaged in acts of violence of a political character, with a political object, and as part of the political movement and rising in which he was taking part.'

There was no evidence that Castioni had any personal grudge against his victim. 'The reasonable presumption is . . . that at the moment Castioni fired the shot . . . he fired it thinking it would advance, and that it was . . . in furtherance of . . . the very object which the rising had taken place to promote, and to get rid of the government.'

Justice Sir Henry Hawkins concurred. He accepted Stephens' definition of a political offence and said: 'The question really is whether this was an act done by this prisoner in his character as a political insurgent at that time.' He held that it was.

He rejected the suggestions that the court should consider whether the killing of Rossi, which he deplored, was essential to the success of the uprising — it clearly was not — or whether the violence used was unreasonable. 'Everybody knows,' he said, 'that there are many acts of a political character done without reason, done against all reason; but at the same time one cannot look too hardly and weigh in golden scales the acts of men hot in their political excitement. We know that in heat and in heated blood men often do things which are against and contrary to reason; but, nonetheless, an act of this description may be done for the purpose of furthering . . . a political rising, even though it is an act which may be deplored and lamented, as even cruel and against all reason, by those who can calmly reflect upon it after the battle is over.'

Justice Stephens concurred as well.

Three years later the principles of the Castioni judgement were reaffirmed and slightly modified in the case of Theodore Meunier. There had been a series of anarchist bombings in France in 1892-3, one of which, at the Cafe Very in Paris, killed two civilians. Meunier a leading French anarchist, fled to Britain and his extradition was sought for the cafe bombing and for a bomb attack on a military barracks.

The case was heard in the Queen's Bench division of the High Court in June 1894. Meunier conceded that the cafe bombing was not a political offence but said the attack on the barracks was. The court rejected his plea, drawing a somewhat questionable distinction between anarchist opposition to government as such and an organised group seeking to overthrow a particular government and replace it with another. But in making this distinction, Lord Justice Cave strongly underlined the basis of the Castioni judgement.[3]

'It appears to me,' he said, 'that in order to constitute an offence of a political character, there must be two or more parties in the state each trying to impose the government of their choice on the other, and that, if the offence is committed by one side or the other in pursuance of that object, it is a political offence, otherwise not. In the present case . . . the party with whom the accused is identified . . . by his own voluntary statement, namely the party of anarchy, is the enemy of all governments. Their efforts are directed primarily against the general body of citizens. They may secondarily and incidentally commit offences against some particular government; but anarchist offences are mainly directed against private citizens.'

Meunier was returned to France for trial where he was found guilty but with extenuating circumstances and jailed for life. His case had also raised another issue very topical in the North of Ireland today. His counsel claimed that the case against him was based on the uncorroborated evidence of an accomplice — i.e. a 'supergrass' — and so was insufficient to secure a conviction.

Lord Justice Cave pointed out that there was some corroboration, but went on to say: 'It is not the law that a prisoner must necessarily be acquitted in the absence of corroborative evidence . . . .' He added, however, 'no doubt it is the practice to warn the jury that they ought not to convict unless they think that the evidence of the accomplice is corroborated . . . .' There were, of course, no juries to warn in the 'supergrass' trials held recently in the North.

By 1895 the political offence exception had been firmly established in English — and therefore Irish — extradition law. The principles involved in determining what constitutes a political offence had been clearly spelt out. The test was whether the offence was 'done in furtherance of . . . with the intention of assistance (in) . . . a political uprising or a dispute between two parties in the state as to which is to have the government in its hands.'

It did not matter whether the act involved was essential to the success of the uprising, or even if it was 'done without reason, done against all reason,' but it was stressed that it must be part of a definite attempt to overthrow one government and replace it with another. It was clearly held that murder and the use of firearms and explosives could all qualify as political offences. Since the two keynote cases had concerned France and Switzerland, the courts clearly felt that the political exception should be upheld even against friendly Western European states with democratic political systems similar to Britain's.

2: From El Salvador to Achill: The Political Exception in the United States

Revolutionary America, like France, welcomed political refugees. Wolfe Tone and other United Irish leaders found shelter there as did the English revolutionary, Tom Paine. The American Declaration of Independence had asserted the right and duty of a people to revolt against what they saw as an unjust government.

It was a sensitive issue in the infant United States. In 1799 President John Adams authorised the surrender to the British naval authorities of Jonathan Robbins, a seaman who was wanted for murder aboard a British naval vessel. There was uproar in Congress. Apparently Robbins was an American who had been press-ganged into the British navy and it was generally believed the murder took place during an attempt at mutiny or escape.

The United States public felt the offence was partly political and that Robbins should not have been surrendered. The controversy helped to bring down President Adams' administration. Feeling remained strong on the issue. In December 1837 William Lyon McKenzie and a few supporters staged a very minor uprising near Toronto in British-controlled Canada, killing a civilian and robbing a stage-coach, then fleeing to the United States. The Governor of New York flatly refused to hand McKenzie over to the British authorities.

When an extradition treaty was signed with Britain in 1842 which made no reference to exemption for political offenders there were protests in Congress. President John Tyler felt obliged to write to Congress saying that the negotiators had not thought it necessary to include a political exception clause because the administration 'held it as a fundamental principle of its Constitution and policy that America would never extradite a man because he had done something in a revolution for his liberty, which in (the requesting) country would be a crime.'

Nevertheless when the United States signed an extradition treaty with France the following year it was stated specifically that it would not apply to 'any crime or offence of a purely political character'.

There was such an influx of economic and political refugees from Ireland after the Famine and the Young Ireland Rising that it could not be long before Ireland figured in a United States extradition case.

In 1852 the British authorities sought the extradition of an Irishman called Thomas Kaine from New York on a charge of attempted murder. Kaine had allegedly fired at a man called James Balfe near Moate, Co. Westmeath. Balfe seems to have taken over land from which another farmer had been evicted. Kaine did not plead directly that it was a political offence, but it caused great excitement and protests in New York and Kaine was not brought to court 'for fear that he would be rescued from the custody of the law by a mob'.[1] In 1853 a circuit court judge ordered his release mainly on the grounds that there was insufficient evidence to establish a *prima facie* case against him.

There were of course much better known fugitives from the Young Ireland movement in the United States, such as John O'Mahony, Michael Doheny, and John Mitchel and Thomas Francis Meagher, who had escaped from imprisonment in Australia, but no action was taken against them. Indeed American sympathy for Irish rebels was such that after the unsuccessful Fenian attempts to invade Canada from the United States in 1867 and 1870, the sum total of the United States authorities' action was to jail the leader of the invasions, General John O'Neill, for six months. The bulk of the invaders returned safely to the United States, but there was no question of them being handed over to Canada.

The Irish question came to the fore again in the 1880s when the Fenians launched a bombing campaign in Britain using the deadly new weapon of dynamite. The dynamite campaign was openly organised and financed from the United States and there was pressure from the British and from conservative elements in America for the Anglo-American extradition treaty to be amended to allow the extradition of dynamiters. Irish-American groups lobbied intensely against the proposed change and when a new treaty was signed in 1889, Article 11 stated specifically: 'A fugitive criminal shall not be surrendered if the offence in respect of which his surrender is demanded be one of a political character . . . .'

In the meantime the concept of the political offence exception had spread south of the Rio Grande as well. In 1888 a conference of Latin American states meeting at Montevideo drew up a draft treaty on international penal law which stated: 'Political offences subversive of the internal and external security of a state, or common offences connected with these, shall not warrant extradition. The determination of the character of the offence . . . shall be made under and according to the provisions of the law which shall prove most favourable to the accused.'

Subsequent Latin American governments observed this principle fairly consistently — if only because heads of government never knew when they might need to avail of it themselves.

So far in the United States there had been no definition of what constituted a political offence. That was to come in 1894, three years after the Castioni decision in Britain, when a California district court refused to extradite General Antonio Ezeta to the Central American republic of El Salvador.

El Salvador was in much the same state of turmoil in the 1890s as it is now in the 1980s. In 1890 General Carlos Ezeta overthrew the government of President Menendez

in a relatively bloodless coup and made himself President
with his brother Antonio as Vice-President and head of the
army. Opinions vary about Ezeta's rule. Some commen-
tators say he was a drunken tyrant, others that he increased
the minimum wage and improved the lot of peasants and
labourers.

The Ezeta brothers were themselves overthrown in 1894
and Antonio and a few companions fled to the United States.
The new Salvadoran government sought their extradition on
charges of murder and armed robbery. The murder was of a
man alleged to have been a spy during the brief, but bloody,
civil war and the bank robbery was to get money to pay
Ezeta's troops while his army was in retreat.

General Ezeta claimed the offences were political. The
United States federal court for California's northern district
held that the crucial questions were whether there was a
political uprising in progress at the time and whether the
offences were incidental to it. The Castioni judgement was
quoted in the case, though this time, of course, the defendant was part of the government *against* which the uprising
was aimed.

Judge Morrow ruled that the acts complained of were
committed during the 'progress of actual hostilities between
the contending forces, wherein General Ezeta and his companions were seeking to maintain the authority of the then
existing government against the active operations of a revolutionary uprising.' Accordingly he held that the offences
were political and ordered that Ezeta and three of his companions should be discharged.[2]

In a passage that was to be as much quoted in the United
States as the Castioni judgement in England, Judge Morrow
said: 'With the merits of this strife I have nothing to do . . .
During its progress crimes may have been committed by the
contending forces of the most atrocious and inhuman character and still the perpetrators of such crimes escape punishment as fugitives beyond the reach of extradition. I have no
authority in this examination to determine what acts are

within the rules of civilised warfare and what are not. War at best is barbarous . . . .'

The court did allow the extradition of one man who was accused of attempted murder four months before the revolt against Ezeta took place, holding that this action was not sufficiently clearly related to the uprising.

Two years later the United States Supreme Court, in what is still its only pronouncement on the political offence exception, adopted the same criteria which had been used in the Ezeta case to determine another political exception plea. In the case of *Ornelas v. Ruiz* in 1896 the Mexican government sought the extradition of members of a band of 140 armed men who had crossed the Rio Grande from Texas into Mexico, attacked a troop of Mexican soldiers and taken over and terrorised a Mexican town for six hours before returning to Texas. They were wanted for murder, arson, robbery and kidnapping.

The defendants claimed their actions were political and evidence was given that some of them had been overheard to talk about fighting the Mexican government. The court noted their speedy return to Texas and the absence of evidence of any sustained campaign against the Mexican government. The judges held that 'the acts of the petitioners were not in aid of a political revolt, an insurrection, or a civil war . . . .' They allowed the extradition.[3]

This second judgement confirmed that the basic element required to successfully plead the political exception was that there must have been a serious political conflict under way at the relevant time and that the offence alleged must have been clearly related to it. The two judgements formed the basis of all future American extradition rulings.

It was not long before these new definitions were put to the test in a remarkable Irish case. In October 1894 Valley House, the home of Mrs Agnes MacDonnell a local landowner, was burned on Achill Island, Co Mayo. Mrs Mac-Donnell herself was attacked and badly beaten. Half her nose was torn off and her skull was fractured.

James Lynchehaun, a thirty-five year old former school-teacher who had worked as an agent for Mrs MacDonnell, was arrested and charged with attempting to murder her. He was convicted and sentenced to life imprisonment. After eight years he escaped from Maryborough (Portlaoise) prison and fled to the United States.

Lynchehaun was arrested in August 1903 in Indianapolis on a warrant seeking his extradition. He claimed the attack on Mrs MacDonnell was part of the Land War between tenants and landowners in Ireland and was a political offence. The local Irish community was worried about the implications of the case for other Irish fugitives. A committee was formed to defend Lynchehaun and 'establish a sacred right', the right of asylum for political offenders.

Lynchehaun was the first convicted prisoner for whom an extradition warrant had been issued. He told the court he had been a member of the Land League and the IRB and the League had planned the attack on Mrs MacDonnell because of her harsh treatment of her tenants. Other Irish witnesses, including some Achill men, reinforced his story. Lawyers for the British government claimed the motive for the attack was purely personal. Mrs MacDonnell had dismissed Lynchehaun as her agent and was about to evict him.

Lynchehaun himself was a ne'erdowell with a violent reputation. In all likelihood his motivation was mainly personal, though others may have been involved and there may have been some Land League connection. But his witnesses convinced the court that there had been a sort of popular uprising against Mrs MacDonnell on the night in question. Lynchehaun's lawyers answered the charge of brutality by comparing the attack on Mrs MacDonnell to the attacks on 'loyalists' who supported Britain during the American revolution and to the less savoury aspects of the French revolution.

United States Comissioner Charles W. Moores, who heard the case, took their point. He described the attack on

Mrs MacDonnell as disgraceful, but said: 'It is not a question of how detestable the acts were . . . . The question is one of law to be determined according to the principles of justice which we find in the courts . . . .'[4]

He accepted the comparison with the French and American revolutions. 'For many years before the war of the revolution the loyalists suffered cruelties unspeakable at the hands of the American colonists. These brutalities form a striking parallel with the acts done by the tenantry in the west of Ireland between 1880 and 1894. . . . A like parallel is found in occurrences preceding the French Revolution. However odious the offences done, there can be no doubt that in the case of the American colonists and the French peasantry, many of the acts were political in their character.'

Lynchehaun's case differed significantly from Castioni and Ezeta because the attack was directed, not at a government or a public official, but at a private individual, and was not directly intended to overthrow a government. His lawyers argued, however, that it was part of a broader movement aimed at changing the political and social order and that in turn it was intimately linked with the struggle for Irish self-government.

Again Commissioner Moores agreed: 'It is evident to me that the assault on Mrs MacDonnell was incidental to, and a part of, a popular disturbance; that the popular disturbance, including the prisoner's part in it, had its origin and cause in a popular movement to overthrow landlordism and was done to further that movement . . . (which) . . . did disturb the political and social order of Ireland . . . in fact, that the riot of 6 October was for political purposes and that its participants were engaged in a partisan conflict whose object was a change of laws and an upsetting of existing political conditions.

'The real test lies deeper than definitions. It is this: Would the crime have been done had there been no political motive? Would the fire and the ensuing riot have occurred

save for the long chain of moving causes that preceded it —
the discontent of the tenants as a class, the agrarian agitation,
the enactment of odious laws, the disagreements of the
various tenants in the island and their landlords, the know-
ledge that the like disagreements existed all over Ireland, the
dispersing of the (IRB) meetings and the arrest of its
speakers . . . . I am convinced that these things were all
moving causes that led up to the climax of October 6 and
that . . . they lent their character to the assault itself.'

He ordered Lynchehaun to be freed.

It was a highly significant judgement which considerably extended the concept of a political uprising and which
certainly indicated that Irish fugitives accused of more
overtly — and genuinely — political offences were unlikely
to be extradited from the United States. Most of the English
papers commented angrily on the judgement while the
Lynchehaun defence committee said it 'establishe(d) the
doctrine that England cannot demand Irish fugitives and have
them extradited without a full enquiry into the original
facts out of which the crime grew and if those facts establish,
according to American notions of liberty, that the alleged
crime was political, extradition will not be granted.'

Flushed with their success and with some money still in
the kitty the defence committee published a pamphlet
giving the speeches of Lynchehaun's attorneys and Commissioner Moores' judgement. They called it *An Irish American victory over Great Britain*.

Lynchehaun's was the last significant Irish extradition case
in the United States until the 1970s. He was by no means
the last wanted Irish man or woman to seek refuge abroad,
however. Indeed a better known refugee was in exile in
Paris at the time *Lynchehaun*'s case was being heard.

Major John MacBride had raised an Irish brigade to fight
on the side of the Boers during the South African war — most
European democrats at the time sympathised with the Boers
in their fight against the British Empire. Few of them knew
anything about the position of the blacks — MacBride was

wanted in Ireland for treason and took refuge in France where he met and married Maud Gonne. He also went on a speaking tour of the United States. He was eventually able to return to Ireland after an amnesty in 1907.

The next prominent Irish fugitive in the United States was Liam Mellowes, who escaped there having led the 1916 Rising in Galway and stayed until 1921 organising arms shipments to Ireland and spending some time in New York's Tombs jail. By then the British seemed to have accepted the impossibility of extraditing Irish rebels. They do not seem to have made any attempt to secure the return of Mellowes or of the best-known fugitive of all.

Eamon de Valera, the President of the underground Irish Republic, escaped from Lincoln jail in England early in 1920 and was smuggled to the United States where he embarked on a near triumphal progress, getting civic receptions and meeting most of the major political figures. He was still officially on the wanted list at home though it is now known that the British government did not really want him arrested as they wanted to keep open the possibility of negotiations with the Irish rebels. Nonetheless, after his return to Ireland he was actually arrested in June 1921 by over-enthusiastic soldiers, just before negotiations began about a Truce. The British government had to hurriedly order his release.

The United States had also provided a much-needed refuge for many humbler members of the Irish revolutionary movement on the run from the British. After the Truce and the Anglo-Irish Treaty in December 1921, these men and women did not have to worry about the British any more, but it was not long before a new stream of Irish political refugees began to arrive in the United States — fugitives from the pro-Treaty victors in the Irish Civil War.

3: 'Quietly Across the Border'

When the British began to pull out of Southern Ireland in 1922 the legal situation was chaotic. British courts and Dáil Éireann courts existed cheek by jowl. The British police force was being disbanded, the Garda Síochána had scarcely begun.

The extradition position was highly confused and the new Provisional Government had every reason to oppose extradition for political offences. The Irish revolutionary movement owed a substantial debt to the principle of the political exception which had allowed many of its leaders to carry on the struggle from abroad when Ireland had become too hot for them. There were sound practical reasons as well for upholding the political exception.

A mutual amnesty had been agreed between Ireland and Britain for all offences committed before the Truce in July 1921. But fighting had continued in the partitioned area of Northern Ireland and a number of prominent figures in the new Dublin administration had been associated with it, such as General Eoin O'Duffy, the chief-of-staff of the new state's forces, and later head of its new police force, General Seán Mac Eoin, one of its senior military commanders and later Minister for Defence, and General Dan Hogan, one of the chief military figures in the border area, and a future chief-of-staff.

There had also been an exodus of Northern IRA members to the South in June 1922 with many of them becoming officers in the Free State army. (They included Seán Haughey, father of the future Fianna Fáil leader, Charles Haughey, and Dan McKenna, who as chief-of-staff of the Irish army during the Emergency, actually revisited the North as the guest of the British Army GOC there.)

Many of these men had reason to fear they were still wanted in the North. That it was not an idle fear was borne out by what happened to Captain Thomas Heuston and Colonel Seamus Woods, both officers in the Free State army.

Heuston, formerly an activist in the IRA in Co. Fermanagh was arrested by the Northern Special Constabulary in November 1922 while crossing a narrow strip of Northern territory en route from Monaghan to Cavan. He was charged with shooting at Northern police in Fermanagh in February 1922 and jailed for 10 years. Even pressure from the British government could not persuade the Northern authorities to release him.

Col Woods, the former commander of the IRA in Belfast, was arrested while visiting his home in Co. Down in December 1923. He was charged with the murder of W.J. Twaddell, a Unionist member of the Northern Ireland parliament, in May 1922, but was eventually acquitted and sent back to the Free State. A number of other Northern IRA men who had joined the Free State army were interned without trial when they strayed across the border in the 1922-3 period.

But both principled and practical objections to extradition for political offences took a back seat when confronted with the cruel realities of the Irish Civil War. An increasingly harsh Free State government had begun executing its opponents without trial. It was not going to let the principles of international law, or even its own 'cold war' with the Northern statelet, stand in the way of getting its hands on its enemies, whether through the legal process or otherwise.

In February 1923 the Southern authorities made approaches to the British government about Frank Aiken, the second in command of the anti-Treaty forces in the Civil War. They claimed that Aiken was evading capture by hiding

out across the border in his native South Armagh and they
wanted Sir James Craig's Northern government to arrest
him and hand him over to them. There was more than a
hint that Aiken would be shot.

A British Home Office official wrote to the British liaison
officer in Belfast saying:

> I had some talk with Craig about Aiken. I am sure the
> Northern government will do everything they can to
> put a stop to his activities. The Free State I gather are
> anxious to have the handling of him. In particular they
> do not want him to be merely interned. Craig gave the
> impression that so far as he is concerned he would be
> quite willing to see him taken quietly across the border
> and delivered to Free State officers.[1]

Aiken was not captured and lived to become the South's
Minister for Defence in the 1930s and 1940s and eventually,
as Minister for External Affairs, to sign the European Convention on Extradition in 1966 on behalf of the Republic
of Ireland. The convention included exemption for political
offenders.

The British authorities were only too happy to facilitate
the Free State government in hunting down its enemies and
around the same time that the Free State was pursuing
Aiken the two governments agreed on a more open handover of political opponents to the Free State, It had an
embarrassing outcome.

On 10 March 1923, using lists supplied by the Dublin
government, the British authorities arrested 59 men and 15
women of Irish extraction in Britain and deported them to
the Free State where they were interned without trial. They
were all opponents of the Treaty and most of them had been
active in Irish support organisations in Britain during the
War of Independence. Some had actually been born in
Britain.

The most prominent of the deportees was Art O'Brien,

president of the Irish Self-Determination League in Britain
and formerly Dáil Éireann's official representative there.
O'Brien's lawyers applied to the British courts for a writ
of *habeas corpus*. The arrest, deportation and internment
of the prisoners had been ordered by the British Home
Secretary, William Bridgeman, under the Restoration of Order in Ireland Act (1920), introduced during the War of
Independence to crush the IRA, and vehemently denounced
at the time by what were now the leaders of the Free State
government.

The Court of Appeal in London on 9 May 1923 held that
O'Brien's arrest was unlawful on the grounds that the Act
had given the power to order internment in Ireland only to
the Chief Secretary for Ireland, whose office had been
abolished; that the setting-up of the Irish Free State had
made the Act inoperative; and that an internment order
could be valid only if the minister who made it retained
full control over the internee and the place of internment —
Bridgeman had no authority or control within the Free
State. The court ordered O'Brien's release.

Lord Justice Scrutton concluded:

> The order of the Secretary of State ordering the intern-
> ment of Art O'Brien in the Irish Free State, in such place
> as the Irish Free State government may determine and
> subject to all the rules and regulations applicable to per-
> sons there interned, was illegal on the following grounds:
> i. That it could only be made under the Regulations
> by a Chief Secretary for Ireland;
> ii. That if (another) Secretary of State had originally
> the power to make it, his power was determined (ended)
> by the setting-up of an Irish Constitution and an Irish
> Executive;
> iii. That there was never any power to order internment
> in a place over which the Government or person issuing
> the order had no control, or to order arrest for the pur-
> pose of such internment. [2]

The British government was forced to hurriedly telegram Dublin and ask for all the deportees to be returned. They were released and London had to pay out over £43,000 in compensation. O'Brien himself was re-arrested in Britain and charged with seditious conspiracy. The Free State authorities supplied evidence against him and he was sentenced to two years in jail. He was released by the British Labour government in July 1924, at the same time as Eamon de Valera was released from prison in the Free State.

With the IRA defeated and demoralised after the Civil War the Free State declared an amnesty and released their IRA prisoners. The Northern authorities released their Republican internees in December 1924 and following the Boundary Agreement between the Free State, Northern Ireland and Britain, the last officially recognised IRA prisoners in Britain and the North were released early in 1926.

In the meantime the legal position about extradition between the Free State, Britain and the North had been sorted out, largely as a result of questions raised by the deportation debacle. Prior to 1922 all Ireland had been part of the United Kingdom although it had a separate police force and judicial system. The arrest and return of offenders between Ireland and other parts of the United Kingdom was governed by the Indictable Offences Act (1848) and — more frequently — by the Petty Sessions (Ireland) Act 1851. The procedure was simple, a warrant issued by a magistrate elsewhere in the United Kingdom was endorsed by the Inspector General or deputy Inspector General of the RIC and could then be executed in Ireland, or vice versa and the accused brought before the court which had issued the warrant.

In April 1923 Kevin O'Higgins, the Free State's Minister for Justice, told the Dáil that under Article 73 of the Free State Constitution, which provided for the continuation of laws and statutes which did not conflict with other provisions of the Constitution, the Indictable Offences and Petty

Sessions (Ireland) Acts were still in force and so the old procedure still applied. The British government made an order expressly extending the provisions of the Acts to cover Northern Ireland.

This backing of warrants procedure contained none of the safeguards normally found in international extradition legislation. In particular there was no political offence exception and no provision for a person arrested under a warrant from outside the jurisdiction to challenge his or her extradition.

That did not cause any immediate problems with Britain, partly because the IRA was not active in Britain again until the late 1930s and partly because the British seem to have refrained from presenting warrants for offences with political overtones. A British Home Office circular in April 1923 had urged great restraint in using the system.

The backing of warrants system worked all right for some years but problems were almost bound to arise in regard to the North, where political tensions were still high. In May 1927 three men, Hugh Rodgers, Frank O'Boyle and William Conlin escaped from Belfast's Crumlin Road jail. Conlin was recaptured but Rodgers and O'Boyle fled to the Free State.

All three had been convicted by a British army court martial in Belfast in April 1921 of murdering a man during an armed robbery near Gilford, Co. Armagh. They had been sentenced to death, commuted to life imprisonment. The three had claimed to be IRA members and had sought release in 1922 when pre-Truce IRA prisoners were freed and again during the general release in 1926 but the Dublin government had refused to acknowledge them.

Rodgers had been a member of the IRB and had been interned in 1916 and Conlin appears to have been in the IRA both in the North and in America. O'Boyle was associated with the IRA and later Fianna Fáil in the South after his escape. The Northern deputy Prime Minister Hugh Pollock told a British Labour minister in 1929 that some people regarded the three as political prisoners.

In December 1928 gardaí called at the homes of O'Boyle and Rodgers in the Free State with warrants issued in the North and endorsed by the Garda Commissioner, General Eoin O'Duffy. The two men got away and in January 1929 they applied to the High Court in Dublin for an injunction restraining O'Duffy and the Attorney-General from arresting them on foot of the Northern warrants.

They claimed to be innocent of the original charge and argued that a conviction by a British army court martial should not be recognised by a Free State court and that the Garda Commissioner had no power to endorse Northern warrants. Their counsel argued that the Petty Session (Ireland) Act 1851 gave no authority for backing warrants from Northern Ireland as that state did not exist at the time the Act was passed and nothing in the Free State Constitution or the Adaptation of Enactments Act authorised the executive to apply the 1851 Act to the North.

It was a politically embarrassing case. It would not look well for the Free State to hand over men who claimed some political involvement and who had been tried by court martial. Justice Meredith gave his ruling in February 1929. He avoided the court martial issue but held there was no authority for extending the jurisdiction of the Petty Sessions (Ireland) Act to include Northern Ireland and so no authority for executing Northern warrants in the Free State.[3] All formal extradition from South to North stopped.

As it happened the Free State government had made an order — the Customs and Excise (Adaptation of Enactments) Order — in March 1924, which provided *inter alia* that all provisions for execution of United Kingdom warrants in Ireland should apply also to warrants from Northern Ireland, but Justice Meredith does not seem to have adverted to this and his ruling was not challenged.

The Northern authorities retaliated quickly, even though a British Order in Council had formally applied the Act to Northern Ireland. They refused to endorse Southern

warrants and the Northern Minister for Education claimed
in the Belfast Senate in 1930 that the legality of executing
Southern warrants in the North was in doubt.[4] There was no
official extradition machinery between North and South for
the next 35 years.

Such a situation was highly inconvenient between two
states with an open land frontier and free passage across the
border. Eventually the gardaí and the RUC began to co-
operate unofficially by simply dumping fugitive offenders
across the border where the local police would be waiting
to pick them up. This arrangement was quite illegal but the
courts on both sides turned a blind eye to it. From the
Southern authorities' point of view it had the advantage of
avoiding political problems. They could pick and choose
whom to return to the North and could avoid political cases.
But presumably they also avoided the bigger more sophisti-
cated criminals who would be more likely to create a fuss
about the whole procedure.

The O'Boyle/Rodgers judgement did not affect the execution of warrants between the Free State and the rest of
the United Kingdom and the system continued to operate
quite smoothly for another 35 years with a minor adjust·
ment in 1938. There was a steady traffic between the two
countries — mostly of persons accused of petty crime and
fraud — with the numbers eventually reaching about 100
each way per year.

Extradition to and from other countries created more
of a dilemma. By 1929 the Free State had sent a number of
extradition warrants to the United States, relying on the
British Extradition Acts 1870-1906 and the treaties concluded under them. But the Department of Justice was un-
easy about the situation and admitted in a memo in October 1929 that the British Acts might not be applicable
to the Free State without a specific resolution of the
Oireachtas. So far no problems had arisen because none
of the Irish fugitives in the United States had been caught
and no other country had sought the extradition of anyone

from Ireland.

The memo concluded:

> . . . it would clear up doubts and would also be more in
> accordance with the policy of the State if our Extra-
> dition relations with foreign States were based on an
> Act of the Oireachtas and on separate agreements with
> the foreign States, rather than on the British Act . . .[5]

An Irish fugitive was caught in the United States in October 1930. William Clifford, a Kerry income tax collector,
was wanted on a charge of embezzling tax monies. The Free
State sought his extradition, relying on the Anglo-American
treaties and it was granted in August 1931. But a memo
from the Department of External Affairs in April 1933,
noted that 'the legal argument was wholly unsatisfactory
and the political reaction from our reliance upon British
Extradition Treaties was embarrassing.'[6]

It was all the more embarrassing because the Fianna Fáil
party — the defeated side in the Civil War — had just come
to power on a platform of dismantling the Anglo-Irish
Treaty and asserting the sovereignty and independence of
the Free State. Moreover Britain had signed a new extradition treaty with the United States in December 1931 to
which the Free State was not a party.

External Affairs had drawn up a draft extradition treaty
with the United States and proposed that treaties be concluded with France, Belgium and Germany as well. The
memo pointed out that a new Extradition Act would have to
be passed to provide the legal basis for the treaties. The
government authorised President de Valera, as Minister for
External Affairs, to negotiate with the United States authorities on the basis of the draft treaty.

A year later External Affairs circulated the heads of an
extradition bill to members of the government. It clearly
spelled out the political offence exception in Section 3:

A fugitive criminal shall not be surrendered (a) if the alleged offence in respect of which his surrender is demanded is of a political character, or if he establishes . . . that the demand for his surrender has in fact been made with a view to punish him for an offence of a political character . . .[7]

The draft provided for a number of other standard safeguards. The requesting state would have to establish that there was a *prima facie* case against the person sought. The accused would have the right to apply for *habeas corpus* in the Irish courts and a person extradited to another country could not be charged with any previous offence other than the one named in the warrant.

The draft also indicated, however, that there would be separate provisions for continuing the existing arrangements with Britain '(which work smoothly and effectively) with such adaptations and amendments . . . as may be necessary or desirable to remove doubts about the legality of the present procedure.' There did not seem to be any intention of introducing the same safeguards for extradition to Britain as for third countries.

The government agreed on 24 March 1934 to go ahead with drawing up the bill, but then hitches seem to have arisen. By December 1938 the bill had still not appeared and an order was made tidying up the backing of warrants procedure with Britain — specifying that the Commissioner and Deputy Commissioner of the Garda were to be regarded as the successors of the Inspector General of the RIC and his deputy. The government was assured the order was purely a temporary measure and the extradition bill would be introduced in the Dáil very shortly. It never was. The Second World War intervened and the whole idea seems to have been shelved.

Meanwhile the IRA — the section that had not joined de Valera's Fianna Fáil party — had gradually re-organised itself and in January 1939 launched a bombing campaign in

England and a series of attacks on the RUC in the North. With the approach of war de Valera felt the IRA's actions in England launched from bases in the South threatened the neutrality of his state and he suppressed them ruthlessly, using legislation similar to that used against himself and his colleagues less than 20 years earlier.

Inevitably the question of extradition arose, but while the Department of Justice drew up a draconian Offences Against the State Act and noted that the absence of extra- dition for IRA-type offences created a 'hiatus' in Irish law, it recognised that extradition could not be used. The argu- ments against were 'mainly of a political character' and if the law was changed it might be 'misunderstood as being done only at the behest of Britain.'[8]

The basic reason why extradition was so firmly ruled out had been summed up in a remark by de Valera to the United States envoy to Dublin in January 1939 when he said the 'great danger' with the IRA and its 'illegitimate methods was that the cause of their violence was legitimate'. Few people in Ireland supported the IRA's bombing cam- paign in England but even fewer supported the idea of handing over IRA members to the government which, they felt, had caused the problem of partition in the first place.

On the other hand the Northern authorities, who had stopped all formal extradition in retaliation for the South's attitude after 1929, and who claimed its legality was in doubt, were not slow to seize an opportunity to get at their traditional enemy, the IRA. A number of IRA men were facing capital charges in the South, following a series of shoot-outs with the Garda Special Branch.

In October 1942 Michael Quille, a Kerry IRA man, was arrested in Belfast. He was wanted on a charge of murdering a garda sergeant in Dublin, a month beforehand — a charge which carried the death penalty. Instead of charging him with some offence in the North or interning him, the RUC took him to the border at Carrickarnon, Co. Louth, and pushed him across the border into the arms of waiting

Garda Special Branch men. Quille was tried by a military court and acquitted but then interned in the Curragh military camp in the South.

In Quille's case no warrant appears to have been issued, it was an entirely unofficial operation. In the case of another man, Harry White, a warrant was issued and executed, however, and he became the only person to be formally extradited from North to South or vice versa between 1929 and 1965.

White was a Belfastman who was wanted for the murder of a Special Branch man in Dublin in October 1942. He had escaped during a shoot-out in which the detective was killed. White's companion, Maurice O'Neill, had been caught at the time, was convicted by a military court and hanged. White had fled back to the North and evaded arrest until October 1946. He was arrested near Derry under the Northern Government's Special Powers Act and held for a couple of days — until the warrant arrived? — then released and re-arrested on a Southern warrant endorsed for execution in the North by the Inspector General of the RUC. He was then taken to the border at Tyholland Co. Monaghan and handed over to the gardaí.

White's lawyers protested about the manner of his arrest in the court in Dublin, but the court held he was lawfully before it and what happened him in the North was not its concern. Lawyers acting for him in the North sought a writ of *habeas corpus* against the Northern Minister of Home Affairs, but the courts held that the Minister did not have custody or control over White so he could not be ordered to produce him. White's lawyers took it to the House of Lords which stood over the Northern court's ruling.

Meanwhile White went on trial in Dublin. He was convicted and sentenced to death by the Special Criminal Court but he appealed — O'Neill had been tried before a military court from which there was no appeal. In February 1947 the appeal court found that the armed detectives who raided the house White and O'Neill were in, had 'no lawful authority

for the intended arrest' of White. They were also in plain
clothes and had not identified themselves.

The court changed the conviction to manslaughter and
commuted the sentence to life imprisonment. White was
released a little over a year later as part of a general amnesty
when the new Inter-party government came into office.

4: 'A Negation of Law and a Denial of Justice'

In March 1946, Eamon O'Neill, a backbench TD asked the Taoiseach in the Dáil what countries the state had extradition agreements with and whether 'refugees from political ill-treatment' were ever sought under these arrangements. De Valera replied: 'Pending the enactment of appropriate legislation . . . no extradition treaties or arrangements have been concluded with other states.' The second part of the question did not arise. He gave no indication that any legislation was planned. The pre-war draft Extradition Bill seemed to have been forgotten about.

Meanwhile the Irish government was firm almost to the point of obtuseness on the question of political offenders — probably a reflection of de Valera's rigid interpretation of wartime neutrality. Towards the end of the Second World War, Ireland like other neutrals, was asked by the Allied powers to give assurances that it would hand over any fugitive war criminals who turned up in its territory. The Irish authorities replied that it was their policy to keep out aliens who would endanger Irish neutrality or good relations with friendly states, but they reserved the right to grant asylum 'should justice, charity or the honour or interest of the nation so require.'[1]

In 1949 Belgium invoked the pre-1922 Anglo-Belgian extradition treaty to request the extradition from Ireland of two men believed to have been involved in the killing of a Belgian nobleman by German SS men and Belgian collaborators. Only one of the men could be found, and in October 1952 the Irish government refused to extradite him, citing the political offence clause of the treaty — thereby implicitly accepting that the pre-1922 treaties were still in operation.[2]

A number of suspected war criminals, mostly smaller fry, took advantage of the government's attitude and passed through or settled down in Ireland. Probably the most significant of these was the former Croatian Interior Minister, Andrija Artukovic, who spent a year in Ireland in 1947 and whose son was born here. He went on to become the subject of the longest-running extradition saga in American history.

The Irish government itself invoked one of the pre-1922 British treaties in 1960 to seek the extradition of a Greek couple from Switzerland — without success. But in general, extradition between Ireland and countries or states other than the United Kingdom did not exist in the post-war years and nothing was done to remedy the situation until the 1960s.

Extradition to and from Britain continued under the Petty Sessions (Ireland) Act 1851 despite the doubts expressed about its legality by the Department of Justice in 1937.

The constitutionality of the 1851 Act was challenged in the Supreme Court in 1950 in the case of John Joseph Duggan, a Kildare man who was sought on an English warrant for defrauding Worcester City Council of £105. Duggan's counsel claimed that the Act was inconsistent with Section 29 of the Constitution which read: 'Ireland accepts the generally recognised principles of international law as its rule of conduct in its relations with other states.'

Their main argument was that it was a principle of international law that extradition laws and treaties should exclude political offences, but the 1851 Act did not. They did not claim the offence for which Duggan was sought was political.

Chief Justice Conor Maguire reviewed a series of extradition laws and treaties between various countries, but took a very precise and narrow view of what constituted a principle of international law — a view that was to be contradicted 24 years later by the Irish representatives on the post-Sunningdale Law Enforcement Commission. The Chief Justice concluded:

> The attempt . . . to establish that the non-surrender of political refugees was a generally recognised principle of international law failed. The furthest that the matter could be put was that international law permitted and favoured the refusal of extradition of persons accused or convicted of offences of a political character, but allowed it to each state to exercise its own judgement as to whether it would grant or refuse extradition in such cases and also as to the limitations which it would impose upon such provisions . . .

The court dismissed Duggan's appeal but acknowledged that the legal position was somewhat unsatisfactory. The Chief Justice concluded: 'The argument that some limitation should be placed on extradition, having regard to the nature of the offence, had force, but . . . if modification was to be made in it, that would be a matter for the legislature.'[3]

The government seemed quite satisfied with the 1851 Act, however, and showed no inclination to change it. Gerald Boland, the Fianna Fáil Minister for Justice said in the Dáil in March 1954: 'I think we should be very slow to upset an arrangement which has stood the test of time and given so little cause for complaint over so long a period.'[4]

After the Harry White case there were no more formal handovers from the North but the informal arrangements continued in non-political cases. As late as January 1962 the RUC dumped a South Armagh man, Michael McWall, across the border into the arms of the gardaí. Questioned about it in the Stormont parliament the Minister of Home Affairs, Brian Faulkner, denied there was any collusion. He said McWall had injured himself escaping from the

gardaí the previous day and the RUC had called to give him
a lift to the doctor's. 'McWall accepted, but on the way to
the doctor's house he decided to change his mind and at a
point near the border he voluntarily walked over into the
Republic and gave himself up to the civic guards.'[5]

Such polite fictions were all very well but the Northern
authorities had been anxious to regularise things for some
time. In May 1952 the Belfast Home Affairs Minister, Brian
Maginess, had complained to his Cabinet about the problems
involved and they had agreed to approach the Southern
government about it. Three years later his successor, G.B.
Hanna, told the Northern parliament that his government was
still anxious to secure a reciprocal agreement. But they got
nowhere, perhaps because tension between North and South
was rising again and the backing of warrants system in operation between Britain and the Republic — which they wished
to extend to the North — had no political exception clause.

In 1953 the IRA had raided a British army training camp
at Felstead in England looking for arms. In 1955 they raided
military barracks at Armagh and Omagh in the North. They
were preparing for a new armed campaign. On 26 November 1955 a smaller Republican group, Saor Uladh, literally
jumped the gun on the IRA and attacked an RUC barracks
in Roslea, Co. Fermanagh, wounding one RUC man. The
raiders retreated across the border into Co. Monaghan.

The Northern premier, Lord Brookeborough, asked Sir
Anthony Eden, the British Prime Minister, to press the
Republic to sign a cross-border extradition agreement. Ulster
Unionist politicians and some of the Belfast papers accused
the Dublin government of allowing its territory to be used as
as a haven by Republican guerrilla groups.

A Fine Gael/Labour coalition government was in power
in Dublin. On 30 November the Taoiseach, John A. Costello,
made a statement to the Dáil on 'Partition and the Unlawful
Use of Force'. He condemned the use of violence by Republican groups, but argued that it was a product of Partition
and of the treatment of the Nationalist minority in the North

over the years.

> One of the evils that have their roots in Partition is that some men's thoughts have turned to force as offering a possible means of bringing Partition to an end. The responsibility for this particular evil rests on the British Government and Parliament which originally devised the expedient of Partition . . . . The responsibility is shared by the subordinate rulers of the Six Counties who have implacably opposed the setting right of this great wrong and have made it all the more bitter by their intolerant treatment of the large Nationalist minority within the area of the Six Counties.[6]

Dealing with extradition calls, the Taoiseach said 'there has never been any serious difficulty about the reciprocal enforcements of warrants in respect of ordinary criminal offences between the British and ourselves . . .' As far as extending this to the North was concerned, legislation would be necessary. 'We see no objection in principle to such legislation applying to persons accused of offences that have no political complexion.' He said it was the British who were holding things up. The Republic wanted to include machinery for the enforcement of maintenance orders in any new legislation but the British did not want to.

But extradition for political offences, notably IRA attacks in the North or Britain, was a different matter. Costello, himself a former Attorney-General, ruled it out with a strong restatement of the political offence exception. 'International law is not a mutual insurance system for the preservation of established governments . . .' he said.

States were bound to prevent the use of their territory for certain types of revolutionary activity against other governments. However, contradicting Chief Justice Maguire's ruling in the *Duggan* case, he continued:

> But this is not to say that international law requires a

state to surrender persons who have engaged in revolutionary activities in another state. On the contrary
it is well settled that every state has the right to grant
asylum to political offenders and to decide for itself
what is a political offence. And it is common form for
every extradition treaty to include a provision specifically excepting political offences . . . . This is no novel
departure but is one of the few principles of international
law that are universally accepted and have never been
seriously challenged.

As far as the Republican attacks in the North were concerned he spelled out his government's attitude very clearly:

I must therefore, emphasise, in order to prevent any
future controversy or discussion on this point, that there
can be no question of our handing over, either to the
British or to the Six-County authorities, persons whom
they may accuse of armed political activities in Britain
or in the Six Counties.

The Taoiseach concluded by again condemning the use of
violence and warning that if it continued, his government
would use 'all the powers and forces at our disposal to bring
such activities effectively to an end.' His attitude could be
summed up thus: paramilitary activity within the Republic
would be rigorously suppressed, but no one would be handed
over to the British or Northern authorities because they
were seen as the cause of the problem in the first place.

The IRA launched its campaign of attacks on the RUC
and public installations in the North at the beginning of
1956. It ran out of steam by the end of 1958 though
sporadic attacks spluttered on until 1962. The coalition
government left office in March 1957, but its Fianna Fáil
successor took the same attitude. IRA members in the South
were arrested and charged under the harsh Offences Against
the State Act or interned without trial, but there was no

extradition.

John A. Costello had referred in his November 1955 speech to a draft convention on extradition which had just been drawn up for the Council of Europe of which the Republic was a founder member. In December 1957 twelve of the Council's member states signed the European Convention on Extradition which came into force in 1960.

The Republic could not sign as it had no basic extradition law, but the government was at last about to get down to drafting one and when it did it was largely based on the European convention. The convention obliged the contracting parties to extradite to each other fugitives wanted for relatively serious offences. It excluded 'political offences' or 'offences connected with political offences' and it had a rule of specialty, i.e. a person extradited could not be charged with an offence other than the one s/he was extradited for — an important safeguard against a person being sought for a non-political offence and then charged with a political one.

But in one respect the safeguards in the convention fell short of those in the British 1870 Act. It did not require the establishment of a *prima facie* case against the accused before s/he could be extradited, whereas the British Act did.

Work on drafting the Irish Act began about 1961. Charles Haughey, Minister for Justice, whose father had been one of the IRA fugitives from the North in 1922, told the Dáil in April 1962 that the reciprocal arrangements with Britain would be updated as well and arrangements made for extradition from and to the North. He stressed that in any arrangements with the North, 'there would of course be no question of departing from the normal international practice . . . in accordance with which extradition for political offences is prohibited.'[7]

An Extradition Bill was introduced in the Dáil in December 1963. Speaking on it in January 1964, Haughey said it was 'almost entirely based' on the principles of the Euro-

pean Convention and he had tried to follow the text of the
convention as far as practicable. There was a brief debate
and then the Bill was deferred because of a case being con-
sidered by the Supreme Court.

The case concerned Philip Anthony Quinn who was
arrested in Dublin on 6 July 1963 on a British warrant
charging him with stealing £3,000 worth of transistor radios
and electrical goods from a London firm. He had just been released from Mountjoy jail in Dublin.

Quinn was incorrectly named in the warrant and he sought
a *habeas corpus* order from the High Court. On 15 July
Garda Inspector Ryan took the unusual step of applying to
the court for Quinn's release, which was granted. Ten or fifteen minutes later Inspector Ryan arrested Quinn on a new
warrant which he had had in his pocket during the court
hearing but had not mentioned to the judge.

Quinn was bundled into a car with two British police
officers and driven to the Border. From there the British
police took him to London that night. In the meantime
the gardaí refused to tell his solicitors where he was. The
whole episode was simply a manoeuvre to prevent him
applying to the courts again.

Quinn's lawyers went to the Supreme Court which ordered
the gardaí to produce him by 19 July, but they pleaded
that he was now beyond their reach. The lawyers then
challenged the constitutionality of his removal, arguing
that the Petty Sessions (Ireland) Act 1851 conflicted with
Article 40, Section 4 of the Constitution because it allowed
the removal of persons arrested without giving them an
opportunity to challenge this in the courts. Article 40, Section 4 provides that persons arrested may complain to the
High Court that their detention is unlawful. By this time
Quinn himself had been convicted and jailed in England.

Counsel for Inspector Ryan and Deputy Garda Com-
missioner Quinn relied on the Supreme Court ruling in *The
State (Duggan) v. Tapley* in 1950 which had found the 1851
Act to be constitutional.

Judgement was given on 31 July 1964. Mr Justice Brian Walsh noted that the constitutional point at issue was different from that in *Duggan*'s case, but he went on to deal with the general argument, drawn from English law, that the court was bound by preceding decisions (the legal doctrine known as *stare decisis*). He took the opportunity to make a classic declaration of the independence of the Irish courts and the difference between their role and that of the British courts on constitutional issues.

> . . . This Court is the creature of the Constitution and is not in any sense the successor in Ireland of the House of Lords . . . I reject the submission that because on the foundation of the State, our courts took over an English legal system and the common law that the Courts must be deemed to have adopted and should now adopt an approach to Constitutional questions conditioned by English judicial methods and English legal training which, despite their undoubted excellence, were not fashioned for interpreting written Constitutions or reviewing the constitutionality of legislation. In this State one would have expected that if the approach of any Court of final appeal was to be held up as an example for this Court to follow, it would more appropriately have been the Supreme Court of the United States . . . This is not to say, however, that the Court would depart from an earlier decision for any but the most compelling reasons. The advantages of *stare decisis* are many and obvious so long as it is remembered that it is a policy and not a binding unalterable rule.[8]

Mr Justice Walsh said that any law to be constitutional must allow a detained person to stay in the jurisdiction long enough to be able to challenge her/his detention in the High Court.

The Chief Justice, Cearbhall Ó Dálaigh, held that Section 29 of the 1851 Act authorised 'removal from the jurisdiction *instanter* without any opportunity, reasonable or otherwise, to invoke the courts'. He ruled that it was 'repugnant to the Constitution and invalid' and added that 'the claim made on behalf of the police to be entitled to arrest a citizen and bundle him out of the jurisdiction before he has an opportunity of considering his rights is the negation of law and a denial of justice'.

He had harsh words for the police officers involved:

> A plan was laid by the police, Irish and British, to remove [Quinn] after his arrest . . . from the area of jurisdiction of our Courts with such dispatch that he would have no opportunity whatever of questioning the validity of the warrant . . . in plain language the purpose of the police plan was to eliminate the Courts and to defeat the rule of law as a factor in Government.

In December 1964 the Supreme Court found Inspector Ryan, Deputy Commissioner Quinn and the two English police officers guilty of contempt of court, but they apologised and no penalty was imposed. As a parting shot the Chief Justice criticised the garda refusal to inform Quinn's solicitor of his whereabouts: 'It is quite intolerable that the legal advisers of a person in custody should be obstructed or misled in their efforts to ascertain the whereabouts of their client.'

The effect of the judgement in *The State (Quinn) v. Ryan* was to stop all backing of English warrants in the Republic. Coincidentally in June 1964 the House of Lords had also ruled that the backing of warrants in Britain under the 1851 Act was invalid. The Lords' decision in *Metropolitan Police Commissioner v. Hammond* ([1964] 2 All E.R. 772) — which sought the extradition of Hammond for alleged neglect of his children — was on the technical ground that there was no British legislation substituting the garda authorities for the RIC in the backing of warrants.

The British authorities were able to remedy this temporarily by an Order in Council but the Irish government could not remedy the unconstitutionality of the Act so readily. For some months there was a big influx of fugitives from Britain into the Republic.

The Supreme Court ruling had made the new Extradition Bill all the more urgent. The first Bill lapsed when a general election was called in the Republic at the beginning of 1965, but it was reintroduced in the Dáil in April 1965 by a new Minister for Justice, Brian Lenihan.

The Bill, which was passed with virtually no changes and became the Extradition Act 1965, had two main sections. Part III dealt with Britain and the North and Part II dealt with extradition to all other states.

Part II followed the European Convention very closely. Extradition could only take place to countries with which a treaty or agreement had been made. Requests for extradition would be made through diplomatic representatives, though in cases of emergency a fugitive could be arrested pending the arrival of the formal request. The suspect would be brought before a District Court and would have fifteen days within which to challenge an extradition order. Fugitives could be extradited only for offences carrying a possible sentence of twelve months or more or if they had been sentenced to four months or more in prison. The offence must correspond to some offence under Irish law and the rule of specialty would apply. There was no requirement to establish a *prima facie* case against the suspect, however.

Section 11 set out the political offence exception:

11. (1) Extradition shall not be granted for an offence which is a political offence or an offence connected with a political offence.
(2) The same rule shall apply if there are substantial grounds for believing that a request for extradition for an ordinary criminal offence has been made for the purpose of prosecuting or punishing a person on account of his race, nationality or political opinion or that the person's

position may be prejudiced for any of these reasons.

Extradition was also prohibited for revenue offences and offences under military law and Irish citizens were not to be extradited unless a treaty or agreement specifically stated otherwise. Irish citizens accused of an offence in another state could be tried in Ireland instead. The Minister for Justice was given power to stop the proceedings at any stage if s/he felt that extradition was prohibited on any grounds.

For Britain and the North (Part III) the procedure was described as the 'endorsement and execution of warrants' rather than extradition and was a good deal less elaborate. In fact it was fairly similar to the 1851 Act, except that it provided that the suspect must be produced before a District Court and be given fifteen days in which to appeal to the High Court. Unlike the procedure for third countries, there was no specialty rule and no restriction on the handing over of Irish citizens. And as in Part II, there was no requirement to establish a *prima facie* case. Brian Lenihan stressed that this part of the Bill had been drafted in close co-operation with the British authorities and a parallel bill, the Backing of Warrants (Republic of Ireland) Bill was currently going through the British parliament.

Part III did contain a political exception clause. Under Section 50 the High Court or the Minister for Justice could order a suspect's release if:

2 . . . (a) the offence to which the warrant relates is —
(i) a political offence or an offence connected with a political offence, or . . .
(b) there are substantial reasons for believing that the person named or described in the warrant will, if removed from the State under this Part, be prosecuted or detained for a political offence or an offence connected with a political offence.

There was a small but significant difference between this

formulation and that in Part II which also prohibited extradition if there were grounds for believing that extraditees might be prosecuted or their position prejudiced on account of their 'race, religion, nationality or political opinion'.

This point was raised when the Bill was first discussed in 1964. Michael J. O'Higgins, a Fine Gael TD — and, ironically, a brother of the Chief Justice who later drastically narrowed the political exception in the case of Dominic McGlinchey — objected to this omission from the section dealing with Britain and the North. He pointed out that the Taoiseach, Seán Lemass, had earlier that day said that discrimination still persisted against the Nationalist minority in the North. O'Higgins also said the requesting state should have to establish that there was a *prima facie* case against a suspect.

The Minister for Justice, Charles Haughey, said the *prima facie* requirement had been dropped because it was not the custom among Continental European countries. And on the question of an extraditee's position being prejudiced he took a position somewhat at variance with his later stance on the North:

> It would be entirely inappropriate for us to suggest that in Northern Ireland or Britain such a qualification or prohibition is necessary . . . It is not an offence under Northern or British law to be a member of a particular religion or of any particular race or to have a particular nationality: it is impossible to envisage a situation where a person would be prosecuted there simply on the ground of being of a particular race, religion or nationality . . .[9]

A couple of Deputies queried the definition of a political offence as it applied to the North. In the first debate on the Bill Patrick McGilligan, a former Fine Gael Attorney-General, raised the question of the killing of RUC members by the IRA and said 'any such killing is murder and could not be excluded on the ground that it is a political offence'.

By the time the Bill was debated again the Taoiseach, Seán

Lemass, had met his Northern counterpart, Captain Terence O'Neill, and there were high hopes of a new climate of good-will between North and South. Michael O'Higgins spoke again but dropped the issue of discrimination and urged that, in view of the new atmosphere, 'offences connected with violence or armed offences, or sorties across the Border, would not be sheltered by us on the basis that these are political offences'.[10]

On the other hand Labour TD Seán Dunne, himself a former member of the IRA who had been interned without trial in the Curragh during the Emergency, warned against premature or hasty gestures with regard to the North. Charles Haughey and Brian Lenihan refused to be drawn on the definition of a political offence saying it should be left to the courts to decide in each individual case.

The Bill went through all its stages quickly and became law in July 1965. Within a year of its passing, on 2 May 1966, the Republic acceded to the European Convention on Extradition. The document was signed by the Minister for External Affairs, Frank Aiken, the former IRA leader whom the Free State authorities were once so keen to get their hands on, regardless of legal niceties.

5: 'The Nett and Only Issue . . .'

The Extradition Act came into force in August 1965. The British Backing of Warrants (Republic of Ireland) Act had come into operation a couple of months earlier. The first person extradited from the Republic under the new Act — though the handover under Part III of the Act was not described as extradition — was John William Bartlett, an Englishman, who was wanted on a charge of breaking into a school in Yorkshire and stealing £3.3s.11d. He consented to be handed over immediately in September 1965.

The first person handed over from the North to the Republic was Martin McDonagh, a 26 year old itinerant, delivered to the gardaí in January 1966 to face a charge of assault and causing grievous bodily harm at Carrick-on-Shannon, Co. Leitrim.

The system worked smoothly enough for the first few years with a steady traffic in each direction of people wanted for fairly routine criminal offences. There were a few fairly unconvincing attempts to plead the political offence exception under Section 50 of the Irish Act.

In 1968 Bernard Rattigan of Ballyhaunis, Co. Mayo, who was wanted on theft charges in Leeds, pleaded that he had been engaged in a PAYE fraud to raise funds for the IRA. Early in 1970 two Englishmen wanted for homosexual offences against a minor, also in Leeds, claimed they were really wanted by the local police Special Branch, for whom they had been acting as informants. And in April 1971 William Lynn Walls, wanted in England on theft charges, told the High Court he was a bishop of the 'Old Roman Church' and had been supplying arms to Catholics in the North. He claimed he was really wanted in connection with that.

The High Court threw out all these pleas, though Walls, who had told the judge he hoped someone would blow him up, was released on a technicality. But it was not long before more weighty claims to the political offence exception were put forward.

The first, not surprisingly, concerned the North. The IRA had finally called off its Border campaign in 1962, but it had not gone away and it staged the odd arms raid afterwards. One was on the British army barracks at Holywood, Co. Down, in 1963.

George Magee, a Belfast garage owner, fled the North in 1964 when he was wanted on charges of house-breaking, malicious damage, assaulting a policeman and driving without insurance. He served a jail term in the Republic in 1967 and was arrested in January 1968 on a Northern warrant.

He claimed that if he was returned to the North he was likely to be charged in connection with the Holywood barracks raid. He told the High Court he repaired cars for British soldiers and had access to the barracks. He had brought another man into the camp who had taken photographs with a view to planning the raid. Magee said he was not a member of the IRA but sympathised with it and was friendly with a lot of IRA members.

The High Court ordered Magee's release in May 1968 but the gardaí appealed to the Supreme Court. Chief Justice Cearbhall Ó Dálaigh gave his judgement in July 1970, making clear *inter alia* that he regarded the activities of the IRA in the North as 'political'. He said: 'In as clear language as perhaps one could expect in the circumstances, Magee has confessed to being concerned in the preparation of an armed IRA raid on Holywood military barracks. There can be little room for doubt that his action falls either within the category of "political offence" or of "offence connected with a political offence".'[1]

Justices Frederick Budd and Brian Walsh assented and

Magee was freed. Mr Justice W. O'B. FitzGerald, supported
by Mr Justice Teevan, disagreed, but not on the question of
whether the raid on the barracks was a political offence.
Mr Justice FitzGerald held that since the return of political
offenders was excluded by the reciprocal British and Irish
legislation, the court should presume that the requesting
authorities would honour that principle 'unless and until
statutes are abused . . .' He did not allow for differing inter-
pretations of what constituted a political offence, however.

On the same day the Supreme Court gave judgement in a
case which had become something of an international *cause
celebre*. In doing so it showed a sturdy disregard for the
likely reaction of not only the Irish, but also the British
government.

In May 1961 George Blake, a British Admiralty employee,
had pleaded guilty in a London court to passing secrets to
the Soviet KGB for the previous nine years. This was the era
of Philby, Burgess and Maclean when it was discovered that
the British secret service and defence establishment were
riddled with spies. In an atmosphere of some hysteria Blake
was sentenced to 42 years in jail.

In Wormwood Scrubs prison Blake met and became friendly with Seán Bourke, a Limerick man. Bourke was serving a
seven year sentence for sending a parcel bomb to a British
policeman because of a personal animosity towards the police.
Bourke was released in July 1966 and three months later he
helped Blake to escape. He hid Blake in London for a while
and then went with him to Moscow.

Bourke got fed up with Moscow, however, and returned to
Limerick where he was arrested in October 1968 on English
warrants for assisting Blake's escape and for sending a
threatening letter to a policeman. He appealed to the High
Court under Section 50 of the Extradition Act, pleading that
it was a political offence or an offence connected with a
political offence. The court agreed and ordered his release
in February 1969. The case had attracted a lot of attention
and there was uproar in Britain. The Attorney-General,

acting for the Irish government, appealed against Bourke's release.

The Supreme Court, by four votes to one, rejected the appeal. Chief Justice Ó Dálaigh's judgement was to stand for a number of years as the clearest and most comprehensive Irish ruling on the political offence exception.

Reviewing the development of the law on the subject, he held that by ruling out extradition for an 'offence connected with a political offence' as well as for a 'political offence', the European Convention on Extradition — on which the Irish Act was modelled — 'has added its protection to a wide area of offences which are not necessarily political in character, but which are simply connected with a political offence.' The 'connected offence' did not itself have to be political in character. 'The Court, in my opinion, should draw the conclusion that the Oireachtas left the connection to be spelt out by the courts in the widest possible manner.'[2]

Bourke had claimed that his motives were political, but he had given a rather confused account of them. He said he was not a Communist and did not support the Soviet Union, but that he agreed with a lot of George Blake's views — Blake was a Communist — and sympathised with him as a political prisoner and one who had been victimised by the British establishment.

The Chief Justice held that Bourke's offence — helping Blake to escape — was not in itself a political offence. But 'Blake's whole object in getting to Russia was to continue in the service of his Soviet master.' His escape was a political offence. 'In my opinion as much so in substance, though not in form, as his original offences under the Official Secrets Act, 1911. In a world divided by ideological difference, Blake's offence was as political as if in war time he had deserted to the enemy lines and changed his uniform. Therefore my conclusion is that Blake's offence in escaping was a political offence and that [Bourke's] offence in assisting that escape was connected with Blake's offence . . . Therefore the plaintiff [Bourke] may not be extradited.'

Mr Justice W. O'B. FitzGerald disagreed once more, holding that Blake's escape was not a political offence.

Chief Justice Ó Dálaigh made some other important points in the course of his judgement. He noted that: 'A distinction can be drawn between "purely" political offences which, of their very nature, are political (e.g. treason, sedition, espionage) and "relative" political offences (e.g. murder) committed in the course of a rebellion.' He indicated that both types of offence were protected under Section 50 of the 1965 Act, making clear in passing that acts of violence, even murder, were not excluded from this protection.

During the High Court hearing an undertaking had been given on behalf of the British Attorney-General that no charges would be preferred against Bourke other than assisting Blake to escape and sending the threatening letter to the policeman. This was to counter a claim that Bourke might be charged with the clearly political offence of harbouring a spy. Chief Justice Ó Dálaigh held that, for a number of reasons — including the possibility of a change in government and a new regime which might not hold itself bound by undertakings given by its predecessors — the Irish courts should not accept or rely on such undertakings.

While the Bourke case was wending its way through the courts the Civil Rights movement had begun in the North. The Catholic/Nationalist minority there had had their hopes and expectations raised by a variety of factors — better education and the welfare state, the relative prosperity of the 1960s, wider horizons encouraged by the television era, and the conciliatory noises made by the new Northern Prime Minister, Captain Terence O'Neill. When there was no change in the system of gerrymandering, repression and discrimination in housing and jobs, they took to the streets in non-violent protest demonstrations.

Civil Rights marches were attacked by the RUC and Loyalist crowds, the RUC invaded the Catholic Bogside area of Derry and in August 1969 the RUC, the B Specials and armed Loyalist civilians attacked Catholic areas in Belfast, burning out dozens of Catholic families. The then Taoiseach, Jack Lynch, said on television: 'The Stormont government is no longer in control of the situation . . . the reunification of the National Territory can provide the only permanent solution for the problem . . .' He called for negotiations with the British government about the future of the Northern state and for the deployment of United Nations troops to keep the peace.[3]

And there was more. The frightened minority wanted protection. Nationalist delegations went to Dublin to ask Lynch's government, which had proclaimed itself their second guarantor, for arms to defend themselves. Money was supplied by the government and arms were bought though they were suddenly intercepted before they reached the North. There was a cabinet crisis in Dublin and two ministers, Charles Haughey and Neil Blaney, were charged with illegally importing arms. They were acquitted amid bitter recriminations over whether the government had officially sanctioned the gun-running. The Northern minority was left confused and disillusioned. The Dublin government had appeared to sanction them arming themselves but had failed to deliver the weapons.

Things got worse. The British army intervened on the streets, welcomed at first as a relief from the Unionist/Protestant RUC and B Specials. There were a few reforms but no UN troops and no negotiations on Irish unity. The British troops were there in 'aid of the civil power' — the Belfast government — and they soon came into conflict with an increasingly angry minority.

The IRA revived and produced a new more militantly Nationalist wing, the Provisionals, which began to attack British troops. The authorities reacted ruthlessly. Nationalists were interned without trial and in January 1972 thirteen civilians were shot dead at a peaceful protest in Derry city. The Nationalist/Catholic population exploded with anger. More and more young Nationalists came to see Irish unity as the only way of escaping Unionist domination, and violence as the only way of achieving it. The IRA was engaged in an all-out conflict with the Northern security forces.

Inevitably fugitives wanted by the Northern authorities for their part in the IRA campaign began to flood across the Border. And the RUC began to issue warrants for them under Part III of the Extradition Act. At first the authorities showed no enthusiasm about enforcing the warrants. The Taoiseach had, after all, declared that the Northern government was no longer in control and he had acknowledged that the position of the minority had become intolerable. The gardaí turned a blind eye to the fugitives or the district courts found some reason to discharge them.

One of the first cases arising out of the Northern Troubles to come before a court was that of three Dungannon men, Edward MacDonald, Thomas McNulty and Edward Hamill, who appeared at Monaghan District Court in September 1971. They were wanted for possession of explosives in Tyrone earlier in the year. The court held there was not sufficient evidence that they were the men named in the warrants and discharged them. Of 32 extradition warrants issued by the Northern authorities in 1971 in connection with 'subversive' activities, and a further 16 in 1972, none had been enforced by October 1972. The Minister for Justice, Des O'Malley, told the Dáil in December 1971 in response to Unionist complaints that the Republic was sheltering gunmen: 'The fact is that extradition for political offences is positively forbidden by the [European] Convention, to which all of us practically in Western Europe . . . have subscribed.'

But the British authorities, who had suspended the local government in the North in March 1972, put more and more pressure on Dublin to act on extradition, making clear it was part of the price they would have to pay if they wanted to be consulted about the future of the North. The Dublin government itself had begun to clamp down very hard on IRA activities within its own jurisdiction, alarmed by a spate of bank robberies and seeing the IRA as a threat to its own position. Des O'Malley revived the non-jury Special Criminal Court for 'subversive' crimes in May 1972 and in December the law was amended to make the unsupported evidence of a garda superintendent to the effect that he believed someone to be a member of the IRA sufficient — if uncontested — to secure a conviction.

The Republic also had some fugitives of its own whom it wanted returned. There had been a £45,000 bank robbery in Dublin in October 1972 and the prime suspects, the Littlejohn brothers, two Englishmen who had been involved with the Official IRA, had fled back to England. Thomas Corrigan, an IRA man who had escaped from the Curragh military prison, had returned to the North. The British and Northern authorities were happy to oblige. The Littlejohns were arrested on an Irish warrant and the Curragh escaper was despatched South again.

In November 1972 two Belfast men, Bernard Elliman and Thomas Fox, were arrested at Shannon on Northern warrants. They had escaped from Belfast's Crumlin Road jail a year earlier while awaiting trial on arms charges. There were protests in Shannon and four Labour TDs accused the government of doing a deal with the British on extradition.

Des O'Malley denied there was any deal and said it would be up to the Courts whether to extradite or not, but from then on there was a steady flow of arrests of Republicans on Northern warrants. Among those detained were the three Tyrone men, MacDonald, McNulty and Hamill, who had been discharged in 1971. This time the district courts ordered the extradition of most of those brought before them, but they then appealed to the High Court either for *habeas corpus* or for the quashing of the extradition order — both on the grounds that their alleged offences were political.

There were some embarrassing moments for the authorities. The Southern government had filed a suit against Britain before the European Court of Human Rights alleging the torture of suspects arrested in the North. When Anthony 'Dutch' Doherty was arrested in January 1973 on a Northern warrant for possession of a revolver in Belfast, his lawyer pointed out

that he was one of the torture victims and the effect of extraditing him would be to hand him back to those who were
alleged to have tortured him.

The appeal procedure was extremely slow and the first
decision in one of the IRA-related cases was not given by the
High Court until December 1973. Anthony Francis Shields, a
45 year old bricklayer from the Lenadoon area of Belfast,
was wanted for possession of nine rounds of ammunition in
October 1971. He had come home on 14 October 1971 to
find a youth had been shot dead in his house by his 16 year
old son. Both youths were in the junior wing of the IRA and
had been handling a gun when it went off. Shields' son was
jailed for manslaughter.

Shields himself was charged with possession of the
ammunition which was found in the house and absconded
while on bail. The history of the High Court proceedings
illustrated the conditions in which some of the refugees were
living at the time. A month earlier the court had dismissed his
appeal when he failed to turn up for the hearing, but had re-
entered it when Shields' solicitor explained he had been un-
able to contact him to tell him it was coming up.

Shields and his family and a number of other refugees had
been living in a large semi-derelict house in Dundrum, Co. Dublin, but the landlord had wanted them out and had removed
the roof. They had had to move and had no fixed address.

Shields admitted to the court that he was a member of an
illegal organisation in the North. He said the RUC had
accused him of being a prominent member of the Official IRA
and had threatened to charge him with attempted murder of
British soldiers. He claimed the offence in the warrant was
political.

Mr Justice Butler was obviously sensitive to the repeated
demands for extradition by British and Northern politicians.
He stressed that the political offence exception was not
peculiar to Ireland but was enshrined in international law. He
said Shields' evidence about his IRA involvement had not
been contradicted and 'he could come to no other conclus-

ion but that the offence charged in this case was a political offence and that if the plaintiff did have possession of the ammunition, it was to be used in the furtherance of IRA activities'. If there was any doubt about it being a political offence, 'he had absolutely no doubt that it was an offence connected with a political offence.'[4]

Two months later, in February 1974, Mr Justice Thomas Finlay (now the Republic's Chief Justice) gave a much more detailed judgement in the High Court in the case of Father Bartholomew Burns, a 38 year old Kerry-born Catholic priest wanted in Scotland on a charge of possessing 130 sticks of gelignite and 150 detonators. It was to remain for almost a decade as the key pronouncement on the political offence exception in relation to the IRA and the Northern Troubles.

Fr Burns had been arrested in Limerick in October 1973 on a Scottish warrant. He admitted the offence, telling the court that he had been working in a Glasgow parish and had become involved in a group working to help Nationalists in the North of Ireland. He felt strongly about the injustices suffered by the Nationalist community and became friendly with a number of IRA members. He was asked to keep the explosives for them and did so.

He said the IRA 'is, and was, engaged in violent political disturbances in Northern Ireland and elsewhere in Great Britain for the purpose . . . of overthrowing British rule in Northern Ireland and changing the political structure and institutions of Northern Ireland.' Accordingly, he claimed that his offence was a political one.

Mr Justice Finlay said: 'The nett and only issue raised for determination by me . . . is whether the safekeeping of explosives for an organisation engaged in an attempt to overthrow and change the political structures of a country by the use of violence . . . is either a political offence or an offence connected with a political offence.'[5]

Keeping the explosives was connected with their ultimate use which was 'intended murder or sabotage'. Noting that Section Three of the Extradition Act excluded the killing of

a head of state or member of her/his family from the category
of political offences, he drew the 'necessary inference that,
were it not for the exclusion, there is at least one type of
murder, or attempted murder, which could or would be a
political offence, and it is clear therefore that one starts at
least with the basis that a political offence is not necessarily
a separate offence from what is described as an ordinary
criminal offence . . .'

He referred back to the definition of a political offence in
the Castioni case as an act 'done in furtherance of, or done
with the intention of, assistance . . . in the course of acting in
a political matter, a political rising, or dispute between two
parties in the state as to which is to have the government in
its hands.' Or again, an act 'incidental to, and form[ing] part
of, a political disturbance'.

Applying these tests, Mr Justice Finlay concluded: 'It
seems to me that the safekeeping of explosives for an organisation attempting to overthrow the state by violence is . . . an
offence of a political character.' And he said: 'It seems again
to me impossible to categorise the existing situation in
Northern Ireland and Britain . . . as being otherwise than a
political disturbance part of and incidental to which is the
keeping of explosives for the organisation known as the IRA.'

Well aware presumably of the attention focused on the
case, especially in Britain, and of the likelihood that he
would be attacked for endorsing 'terrorism', Mr Justice
Finlay added: 'I am not entitled or requested to pass any
value judgement on the organisation with which the plaintiff
says he was in sympathy and for which [he] says he carried
out this storage of explosives. I am not required to express
any point of view as to whether the activities have any likelihood of success or whether they are wise or justifiable. I am
asked a simple question and that is, on the facts as they have
been proved, was this a political offence?'

His answer, based on the legal authorities, was yes. But he
added, letting a shaft of daylight in among the dusty law
books: 'If it were required to aid that legal decision with a

common sense appraisal of what the meaning of political
offence were, it would be difficult to avoid the same conclusion.' He ordered Fr Burns to be discharged.

The state did not contest the Burns decision and for almost
a decade afterwards a series of extradition cases came before
the High Court with the plaintiffs claiming that the offences
in the warrants — possession of firearms or explosives, murder
or attempted murder — were carried out as part of the IRA's
campaign of violence and so were political offences. They
were all discharged with counsel for the Attorney-General
sometimes conceding in court that the offences were political.

One other case merits more detailed notice — that of
Mrs Roisín McLaughlin, a 30 year old Belfast civil servant.
Mrs McLaughlin was arrested in Cork in May 1973 on a
warrant alleging the murder of a British soldier in Belfast two
months earlier.

It was a gruesome case. Four unarmed off-duty British soldiers were lured to a flat on Belfast's Antrim Road by a
group of women. While they were there gunmen burst in and
shot them. Three died, one survived. The RUC were alleging
that Mrs McLaughlin was one of the women involved.

Her appeal was heard by Mr Justice Finlay in December
1974. It was unusual because she did not give evidence and
neither admitted nor denied the offence so there was not the
usual statement of motive before the court. Her counsel,
Anthony Hederman SC, said he did not call her because 'she
could not be compelled in any way to commit herself' in
regard to a murder charge.

(Ten years later, in 1984, Hederman as a judge of the Supreme Court was to reverse that view when Seamus Shannon
pleaded that the murder of Sir Norman Stronge and his son
in Co. Armagh in 1981 was a political offence. Shannon
denied the offence and Mr Justice Hederman held that it was
impossible to rule that an offence was political unless the
plaintiff admitted involvement, as it was the motive of the
perpetrator which was the deciding factor.)

Roisín McLaughlin's husband gave evidence that the RUC

had informed him that they believed she was an intelligence officer in the IRA and had been involved in the killings in that capacity.

Mr Justice Finlay said that considering the degree of organisation, the number of people involved, and the fact that it was clearly intended to kill all four soldiers, it was unlikely that the motive was personal revenge, robbery, or passion.

'There could be no doubt that even murder, and even such a dastardly murder as that described . . . in this case, if carried out by an organisation which, by such methods, sought to overthrow the government of a country by force, was a political offence.' On the evidence he 'must conclude that there was no other really possible explanation of the murder . . .'[6] He discharged Mrs McLaughlin under Section 50 of the Extradition Act.

The political offence exception now seemed securely entrenched in Irish extradition law. In December 1975 the Irish Minister for Justice, Mr Patrick Cooney, told the Dáil that since 1969 404 people had been handed over to Britain and 52 to the North under Part III of the Extradition Act. But earlier in the year the British Lord Chancellor had told the House of Lords that not one person had been extradited from the Republic for 'terrorist-type' offences.

6: 'Detrimental to have Such People at Large . . .'

The pressure by the British government and the Unionist parties in the North for extradition from the Republic had continued and even increased after the suspension of the Northern government in March 1972. The British authorities had been trying to put together a coalition administration in the North which would defuse the revolt of the Nationalist/ Catholic minority by giving some of them a share in power for the first time since the state was set up. The Republic would also be given a nominal role in Northern affairs but part of the price of this would be extradition or some other action against IRA fugitives in the South.

In October 1973 the Unionist Party, the Alliance Party — a non-sectarian pro-Union group — and the Social Democratic and Labour Party (SDLP), which had become the main 'constitutional' Nationalist party, agreed in principle to form a joint administration in the North. In December 1973 they met the leaders of the British and Irish governments at Sunningdale in England to finalise a package deal. A Council of Ireland would link the new 'power-sharing' Executive in the North with the Republic and there was a vague proposal for all-Ireland control of policing in the future.

In return the Dublin government — now a coalition dominated by the traditionally less nationalist Fine Gael party — declared there could be no change in the constitutional position of Northern Ireland unless a majority there consented to it. That in itself was a significant shift from the traditional position of all parties in the South that a minority of the population of the national territory — the Ulster Unionists —

had no right to veto the wishes of the national majority. But the Dublin delegation also agreed 'that persons committing crimes of violence, however motivated, in any part of Ireland should be brought to trial irrespective of the part of Ireland in which they are located.'

They had been pressed hard by the British and the Unionist and Alliance Party representatives to simply agree to extradition, but had argued that the political offence exception was 'a well-recognised principle of international law', from which they could not depart. The Sunningdale conference agreed to set up a joint Law Enforcement Commission to consider the question. Meanwhile the power-sharing Executive took office in Belfast on 1 January 1974.

The eight commission members, four from the Republic and four from the United Kingdom, included Mr Justice Brian Walsh of the Republic's Supreme Court and Mr Justice Seamus Henchy of the High Court, together with Lord Justice Scarman from the British Law Lords and the North's Lord Chief Justice, Sir Robert Lowry. They reported in April 1974.

The report did not beat about the bush. Extradition for other offenders worked satisfactorily so what they were concerned about was 'fugitive political offenders'. The commission members drew up a schedule of offences they wanted to deal with — murder, manslaughter, explosives and firearms offences, malicious damage, robbery, kidnapping, hijacking and escaping from custody. They discussed four possible methods of dealing with fugitives: an all-Ireland court and common law enforcement area; modifying the political offence exception to allow extradition for offences connected with the Northern Troubles; extra-territoriality — i.e. giving the courts in each area power to try offences committed in the other area; and extra-territoriality with mixed courts, where at least one of three judges hearing a case would always come from the other jurisdiction.[1]

All the proposals involved acceptance by the Southern courts that politically-motivated violence against the Northern state was a criminal offence and, to a greater or lesser degree, they all involved endorsement of the North's judicial and law enforcement system. Indeed Paragraph 38(c) of the report said '. . . politically motivated offences of violence are, in effect, offences . . . against the island as a whole irrespective of the jurisdiction in which they are committed'. The pay-off and unspoken justification for this was the inclusion of Catholics and Nationalists in the Northern Executive and the establishment of a Council of Ireland.

Both sides of the commission rejected the idea of all-Ireland courts. It would have involved amending the Republic's Constitution and would have taken too long to set up. It might well have proved unacceptable to Ulster Unionists as well, but that aspect was not discussed.

The Irish team rejected extradition of 'fugitive political offenders' in a long and detailed chapter — though Mr Justice Henchy distanced himself from his colleagues, saying he opposed extradition only because he could not be certain that it would not be ruled unconstitutional.

The Irish delegation pointed to Article 29(3) of the Constitution, laying down that 'Ireland accepts the generally recognised principles of international law as its rule of conduct in its relations with other states'. They argued that non-extradition of political offenders was such a principle.

Every international convention dealing with extradition of which we are aware recognises the existence of the principle of non-extradition for political offences . . . there is overwhelming evidence to support the view that both by international custom, as evidenced by the general practice accepted as law, and by international conventions, both general and particular, it is a generally recognised principle of international law that extradition is not granted for political offences.

This was at odds with the ruling of the then Chief Justice in the case of *The State (Duggan) v. Tapley* [1952] I.R.62

but the Irish team argued that Chief Justice Conor Maguire's
ruling then had been wrong and that the political exception
had become even more entrenched since then, especially
since the adoption of the European Convention on Extradition and the Republic's adherence to it in 1966.

Accordingly they said:

> These members cannot advise that the Government of
> Ireland could legally enter into any agreement or that the
> legislature could validly enact any legislation affecting its
> relation with other states which would be in breach of
> the generally recognised principles of international law.
> For as long as those generally recognised principles forbid
> the extradition of persons charged with or convicted of
> political offences, these members cannot advise that any
> agreement or legislation designed to produce this result
> would be valid.

They also argued that to extradite political offenders
would be in breach of the European Convention on Extradition.

The British and Northern side argued that while non-
extradition for political offenders was 'a widespread and well-
accepted practice', it was not a *principle* of international law.
In a rather patronising passage, they disputed the Irish team's
interpretation of the Republic's Constitution, arguing that
Article 29.3 provided only that Ireland should be *guided* by
the rules of international law. They cleverly cited a judgement by Mr Justice Henchy to reinforce their claim.

The commission reached an impasse on extradition, but the
Irish side agreed to support a scheme of extra-territorial jurisdiction and the British and Northern representatives accepted
it as second-best. Neither side saw much advantage in having
mixed courts and they felt they would only attract hostile
attention. The report recommended the extra-territorial
solution, but urged that it be limited to the offences listed in
the schedule and 'that it be applied only to those who are

believed to be fugitive political offenders'.

It seemed strange that the British, who had originally been among the strongest upholders of the political exception, were now so ready to abandon it, but the attitude of the British courts had changed significantly in the previous twenty years. At first in *Kolczynski's* case they had broadened the definition of a political offence.

In 1954 seven sailors on a Polish fishing trawler had mutinied, overpowered their captain and taken the ship into an English port. Poland sought their extradition under a pre-war treaty with Britain. The sailors claimed their offence was political. A political officer on the ship had been spying on them and they had feared that when the trawler returned to Poland they would be charged with political crimes.

This was not part of, or incidental to, a political rising or a dispute between two parties in the state as to which should have the government in its hands, the criteria laid down in the Castioni and Meunier cases. But the Cold War was at its height at the time and the court was influenced by the prevailing anti-Communist attitudes to broaden its approach, allowing considerations about the legal system in the requesting country to influence its decision.

The Lord Chief Justice of England, Lord Goddard, said: 'The evidence about the law prevalent in the Republic of Poland today shows that it is necessary, if only for reasons of humanity, to give a wider and more generous meaning to the words we are now construing, which we can do without in any way encouraging the idea that ordinary crimes which have no political significance will be thereby excused.'[2] The sailors were not returned.

But in 1962 in *Schtraks'* case the House of Lords had narrowed the definition again, making it seem more restrictive than in Castioni and Meunier. Schtraks was an Orthodox Jew in Israel who abducted his young nephew from the child's parents because they would not bring him up in the Orthodox manner. He fled to Britain and the Israeli authorities sought his extradition. There was a lot of political con-

troversy about the issue in Israel and Schtraks claimed it was
a political offence.

The House of Lords rejected his claim and Viscount Radcliffe introduced a new element into the definition of a
political offence. He appeared to suggest that the key
element was the motive of the requesting government. It was
only if it sought the return of fugitives in order to punish
them for their political views that the offence could be
regarded as political.

> In my opinion the idea that lies behind the phrase
> 'offence of a political character' is that the fugitive is at
> odds with the State that applies for his extradition on
> some issue connected with the political control or govern-
> ment of the country . . . It does not indicate, I think, that
> the requesting State is after him for reasons other than
> the enforcement of the criminal law in its ordinary, what
> I may call its common or international, aspect . . . it
> would be lost sight of, I think, if one were to say that all
> offences were political offences so long as they could be
> shown to have been committed for a political object or
> with a political motive or for the furtherance of some
> political cause or campaign. There may for instance be all
> sorts of contending political organisations or forces in a
> country and members of them may commit all sorts of
> infractions of the criminal law in the belief that by so
> doing they will further their political ends: but if the
> central government stands apart and is concerned only to
> enforce the criminal law that has been violated by these
> contestants, I see no reason why fugitives should be pro-
> tected by this country . . . on the ground that they are
> political offenders.[3]

Significantly Mr Justice Finlay explicitly rejected this line
of argument in the Republic's High Court in *Burns v. Attorney General* in 1974, saying: 'If [Viscount Radcliffe's judge-
ment] is to be construed as imposing on a court the obligat-

ion of trying to . . . ascertain whether the [requesting] state merely wants to enforce its criminal law or seeks to enforce it with some regard to a particular political issue, I would find it an impossible task and one not warranted by the Extradition Act . . .'

Ten years later United States judge John Sprizzo raised the question of whether the British government could be said to be neutral in the Northern Ireland conflict . . . 'because it is the end of British rule in Ireland that has been and continues to be the principal objective of the Irish Republican Movement.' Judge Sprizzo was giving judgement on an application by the British government for the extradition of a Belfast IRA man, Joseph Doherty.[4]

At any rate, following the Schtraks decision the British courts had adopted a very narrow interpretation of the phrase in the 1870 Act, 'offence of a political character'. Of course the British Act did not contain the additional phrase present in the Irish Act, 'an offence connected with a political offence'.

By 1974 the British courts had actually dealt with a number of cases of extradition to the Republic where the fugitive had raised the political exception. The first case was that of Padraic Dwyer who was wanted on a charge of shooting at gardaí in Dublin in 1968 and who had jumped bail and fled to England. He said he was a member of a small Republican armed group, and the offence was political. The court of Queen's Bench rejected his plea in March 1970.[5]

In the second case the Republic sought the return of Frank Keane, wanted on a charge of armed robbery at Rathdrum, Co. Wicklow and of the murder of a garda during a robbery in Dublin in April 1970. Keane was a member of Saor Eire, another small Republican group. He did not claim that the killing of the garda was political, but said that if he was returned he might be charged with political offences. The case went to the House of Lords in March 1971 which rejected Keane's claim largely because he was not 'at odds' with the requesting government.[6] All the fugitives from the Republic faced the problem that there was no evidence of widespread disturbances or an uprising against the government there, as there was in the North of Ireland.

Keane was extradited but was acquitted of both charges in Ireland.

In February 1973 the court of Queen's Bench in London had rejected pleas by Keith and Kenneth Littlejohn that they should not be returned to Dublin to face charges of robbing a bank in Dublin's Grafton Street because it was a political offence. The Littlejohns had claimed they were employed by the British government to infiltrate the Official IRA in the South and robbing the bank was part of their cover. They attempted to summon the British Foreign Secretary and some junior ministers as witnesses but they did not appear and the case was heard in camera. The Lord Chief Justice, Lord Widgery, agreed the Littlejohns had joined the IRA for 'somewhat unconventional motives', but held that there was not enough evidence to show that the robbery was politically motivated.[7] It would of course have been very embarrassing to the British government had the court accepted the Littlejohns' story.

The brothers were returned to Ireland where they were convicted and jailed. Kenneth Littlejohn escaped and fled to England in 1974, but was re-arrested and returned in 1975 after another unsuccessful plea.

The last of these cases was that of Robert Taylor, an 18 year old member of the Northern Loyalist paramilitary group, the Ulster Defence Association. He was sought by the Republic in connection with the murder of a young engaged couple, Oliver Boyce and Breege Porter, who were shot dead on their way home from a dance in Co. Donegal on New Year's morning 1973. Taylor's counsel claimed that Boyce was killed because he was a member of the IRA and so the offence was political, but the Northern Ireland High Court rejected the plea on the ground that no previous judicial pronouncement supported a definition of a political offence wide enough to cover this. It also rejected the suggestion

that Taylor would not get a fair trial before the jury-less
Special Criminal Court in the South.[8]

Ironically Rev. Ian Paisley and other Northern Loyalist
politicians, who had so vehemently demanded extradition
from the Republic, protested loudly at the handing over of
Taylor in June 1973. He was acquitted in Dublin in September 1973 when the court ruled that a confession he made to
the RUC was not made voluntarily.

By the time the Law Enforcement Commission had been set
up the British courts had left very little scope for pleading
the political exception within their jurisdiction. But the Irish
courts had not followed that path and Mr Justice Finlay had
explicitly rejected it in *Burns'* case (see above). Hence the
sharp division on extradition and the fact that the most the
Irish members of the Law Enforcement Commission would
agree to under pressure was the extra-territorial jurisdiction.

But just one month after the commission reported, the
power-sharing Executive in the North was brought down by
a work stoppage organised by hardline Unionist politicians
and Loyalist paramilitary groups. The experiment of allowing Catholics or Nationalists a share in power had lasted just
five months and the Council of Ireland had not got off the
ground at all.

The main ingredient of the Sunningdale package had gone
and it might have been expected that the recommendations
of the Law Enforcement Commission would have been
shelved as well. But the Northern Troubles had been making
an ever greater impact in the South. During the Loyalist
stoppage which brought down the power-sharing Executive
Loyalist groups had planted bombs in Dublin and Monaghan
which had killed 33 people. IRA members had killed a member of the Republic's Senate, Billy Fox, in March 1974. The
spate of armed robberies had continued unabated while the
cost to the Republic of increased security on the Border was
mounting steadily.

The Coalition government in Dublin, headed by Liam Cosgrave, seemed to abandon hope of any political solution in the North in the short term and opted instead for a tough security clampdown in tandem with the British authorities in an attempt to crush the IRA. The government appeared to reverse the position taken by the previous Coalition Taoiseach, John A. Costello, in 1955, when he argued that IRA violence was the product of partition and the oppression of the minority in the North. The logical conclusion of that had been that violence was likely to continue until its causes were removed.

Liam Cosgrave summed up the changed outlook of his government two years after the fall of the Northern Executive when he said:

> The principal element in the conflict is undeniably the armed campaign of violence conducted by the IRA against the security forces and against the economy and life of the area . . . We have also recognised that the prospects of securing agreement on a form of government to which both sections of the Northern community would give their allegiance would be greatly enhanced if the incidence of violence could be reduced and ultimately eliminated.[9]

He was introducing a motion to declare a state of National Emergency so as to take yet tougher measures against the IRA.

At any rate the Coalition decided to go ahead with implementing the recommendations of the Law Enforcement Commission, powersharing or no powersharing. The Criminal Law Jurisdiction Bill was introduced in the Dáil in November 1974.

The kernel of the Bill was Section 2(1): 'Where a person does in Northern Ireland an act that, if done in the State, would constitute an offence specified in the Schedule, he shall be guilty of an offence and he shall be liable on conviction on indictment to the penalty to which he would have been liable if he had done the act in the State.' The schedule was essentially the same as that in the commission's report.

An obvious problem about the scheme was that witnesses to an offence in the North, whether members of the security forces or civilians, might be reluctant to go to the Republic to give evidence. The Bill provided for evidence taken before a High Court judge in the North to be admissible in Southern proceedings and vice versa. (There was provision for the judge trying the case and the defendant to be present for the taking of this evidence.) It also took the opportunity to substantially increase penalties for a number of offences, whether committed North or South of the Border, and it amended the Explosives Act to make it an offence for an Irish citizen to cause or conspire to cause an explosion outside the state. This effectively extended the scope of the Bill to cover bombings in Britain as well as in the North.

The Bill had a peculiar passage. After its introduction in the Dáil nothing more was heard of it until April 1975 when the Minister for Justice, Patrick Cooney, suddenly withdrew it from the Dáil and introduced it in the Seanad where the government had a much bigger majority. Eventually it returned to the Dáil in November 1975, by which stage a reciprocal Act covering the North had been passed by the British parliament.

Moving the Bill in the Dáil Patrick Cooney made no reference to the political causes of the Northern violence, nor to the political reasons for refusing to extradite 'fugitive political offenders'. He referred vaguely to 'legal constraints' on extradition and then said: 'It is detrimental to us to have such people at large in our society. In addition it is a matter of grave scandal in Northern Ireland that fugitive offenders can find safe refuge in our jurisdiction.'[10]

Nonetheless, he stressed that 'the Bill does not provide another form of extradition for those who have escaped that process. For all its tough law and order attitudes, the Coalition government was still not prepared to tamper with the political offence exception to extradition.

The Bill was strongly opposed by the Fianna Fáil party who claimed it was unworkable, inconsistent with the European Convention on Human Rights, and probably unconstitutional. They urged instead the establishment of all-Ireland courts. Former Taoiseach Jack Lynch described the Bill as a futile gesture which would only bring the law and courts in the Republic into disrepute. Major Vivion de Valera (son of Eamon de Valera) had put it more strongly earlier in the Bill's passage, saying: 'We are worried about . . . your attempts to sell out to the British.'[11]

The second reading was carried in the Dáil by 69 votes to 67. The Bill was referred to the Supreme Court which ruled that it was in accord with the Constitution and it became law in May 1976.

The Coalition government, which seemed to some observers to have become paranoid about security, went on to enact ever harsher measures, including in September 1976, a declaration of a state of emergency and an accompanying Act giving the gardaí power to detain suspects for seven days. The Minister for Posts and Telegraphs, Dr Conor Cruise O'Brien seemed to be moving towards censorship of the press. There were repeated allegations that a 'heavy gang' within the gardaí were beating suspected 'subversives' into signing confessions and in June 1977 Amnesty International sent a mission to the Republic which found evidence of maltreatment of suspects by the gardaí.

But despite its tough security policies, the Coalition refused to sign a new European Convention on the Suppression of Terrorism adopted by most member states of the Council of Europe in January 1977. The government refused because the convention effectively sought to put an end to the political exception to extradition for all offences involving violence. Article One of the convention said:

> For the purposes of extradition between Contracting States, none of the following offences shall be regarded as a political offence, or as an offence connected with

a political offence, or as an offence inspired by political motives.

The list included, as well as international offences like aircraft hijacking and offences directed solely against civilians like kidnapping or taking hostages, any 'offence involving the use of a bomb, grenade, rocket, automatic firearm or letter or parcel bomb if this use endangers persons.' Article Two said the contracting states could also exclude any

> serious offence involving an act of violence . . . against the life, physical integrity or liberty of a person . . . an act against property . . . if the act created a collective danger for persons.

No distinction was made between attacks on civilians, attacks on government or political leaders, or attacks on security forces. The convention effectively ruled out any form of armed political resistance to established governments. Ironically many of the contracting parties were countries where such resistance had flourished during the Second World War or, even, in the case of Cyprus, in the 1950s against the British. Indeed, apart from the United Kingdom, armed resistance was still going on in one other contracting party, Turkey, in circumstances which many Europeans would have thought justifiable.

The convention had its origins in the early and mid-seventies when there had been a spate of aircraft hijackings and multiple killings by Palestinian splinter groups (e.g. at the Munich Olympic Games and at Lod Airport in Israel in 1972) and attacks by small, unrepresentative urban guerrilla groups like the Baader-Meinhof group in West Germany and the Red Brigades in Italy. Western European governments seem to have panicked, over-estimating the threat from what proved to be a fairly temporary phenomenon.

At any rate the Coalition government and the Fianna

Fáil administration which succeeded it in the middle of 1977 both refused to accede to the Terrorism Convention. Subsequent governments held firmly to that position, even when EEC Ministers meeting in Dublin in 1979 signed an agreement to step up security co-operation under the convention.

The Dublin governments followed the line of the Irish representatives on the Law Enforcement Commission, simply arguing that it would be unconstitutional to extradite political offenders. They avoided the broader political arguments which underlay their reluctance to extradite to the North — either John A. Costello's argument that it was partition and Unionist policies which caused the violence or another argument that was gaining ground in the Republic, distrust of the Northern law enforcement system.

That distrust was born of the partisan actions of the RUC, British army and UDR in the earlier part of the Troubles. It was reinforced in September 1976 when the European Commission on Human Rights found that 12 men 'interrogated in depth' when internment was introduced in the North in 1971 had been tortured. The European Court reduced this finding in 1978 to 'inhuman and degrading treatment', but it was still enough to discredit the Northern authorities' methods of securing information.[12]

Any tendency to believe such methods had been abandoned was dispelled in June 1978 when Amnesty International found there was evidence of serious ill-treatment of detainees at the RUC interrogation centre at Castlereagh, where large numbers of suspects had been induced to sign confessions. An official enquiry set up by the British government itself confirmed in 1979 that detainees in the North had suffered serious injuries while in RUC custody.[13] These reports reinforced the strong popular opposition to extradition in the Republic.

In the meantime the Criminal Law Jurisdiction Act had come into operation in June 1976. Despite the frequent Unionist complaints that the South was awash with unextra-

dited offenders the British and Northern authorities were
very slow to use the new measure. The first prosecution
under it in the Republic was not taken until 1980. James
Lynagh, Aidan McGuirk and Lawrence McNally were charged
with the murder of Henry Livingston, a former member of
the UDR, at Tynan, Co. Armagh in March 1980. The three
men were tried before the Special Criminal Court in Dublin
in July and RUC men travelled South to give evidence. The
case was dismissed for lack of evidence.

The first convictions under the Act did not come until
December 1981 when Robert Campbell and Michael Ryan,
who had broken out of Crumlin Road jail in Belfast in July
1981, were convicted of escaping from custody and shooting
at the RUC during their escape. They were sentenced to 10
years in jail in the Republic. In February 1982 four more
Crumlin Road escapers were convicted and in July 1982
Gerard Tuite who had escaped from Brixton prison in London was convicted of possessing explosives in London three
years earlier. He was sentenced to ten years as well.

Only one case was heard in the North. Owen Macartan
Smyth, a Monaghan publican, was charged with counselling
and procuring — in Monaghan — the murder of Sir Norman
and James Stronge across the Border at Tynan, Co. Armagh,
in January 1981. He was tried in May 1982 and evidence was
taken in the South with Macartan Smyth and his Northern
judge in attendance. He was acquitted of the murder but convicted of IRA membership.

All in all only 13 prosecutions have been taken in the
Republic since the Act was passed. They reached a peak in
1982 with five prosecutions. There were only two cases in
1983 and none in 1984. Evidence for prosecutions in the
South must be furnished by the Northern authorities and
Southern legal sources have repeatedly claimed that the
Northerners have failed to provide the evidence for more
charges to be laid. The implications seem clear — either the
Northern authorities do not have evidence against as many
suspects in the South as they claim, or they do not want to

use the Criminal Law Jurisdiction Act and prefer instead to continue calling for extradition of Republican fugitives.

The preference for extradition suggests either that it is seen as a political prize to please the Ulster Unionists or that the authorities in Belfast are not sure that courts in the Republic would convict suspects as readily as Northern courts would on the type of evidence offered to them.

7: 'The Obvious and Inescapable Conclusion'

The United States had been the traditional refuge of Irish political fugitives from the 1798 Rebellion to the aftermath of the Civil War. Things were no different after 1945. IRA members who had been active in the 1940s and 1950s military campaigns made their way to the United States as well. The leaders of both the Republican guerrilla groups involved in the 1950s — Seán Cronin, chief-of-staff of the IRA, and Liam Kelly, head of Saor Uladh — went to America when the campaign petered out.

No attempt was made to extradite any of these fugitives. The political offence exception had become well established in United States law. The United States courts had maintained and strengthened the tradition of the political exception since the Ezeta and Lynchehaun cases at the turn of the century. In the Cold War hysteria of the 1950s they had even extended it to cover acts that most people would regard as war crimes and genocide in a case where the perpetrator was sought by a Communist government.

In 1952 President Tito's government in Yugoslavia sought the extradition of Andrija Artukovic, Minister of the Interior in the puppet regime established by the Nazis in Croatia during the Second World War. Artukovic was accused of the slaughter of about half a million Jews, gypsies, Communists and other opponents of the Croatian regime. He had escaped to the United States via Switzerland and Ireland, where he had spent a year living under an assumed name in 1947-48.

Artukovic pleaded that the offences were political. In a long series of hearings which lasted until 1959 a succession of courts upheld Artukovic's claim on the grounds that the killings occurred at a time 'when various factions representing different theories of government were struggling for power in Croatia'. Extradition was refused. Ironically it was the second time Artukovic had benefited from the political exception. In 1934 he had been one of a group of Croatian nationalists who had assassinated the King of Yugoslavia in Marseilles in France, killing the French Prime Minister in the process. They fled to Italy where Mussolini refused to extradite them on the grounds that it was a political offence.

The Artukovic case was an extreme one and was influenced by the political climate of the time, but the judgement in the final hearing summed up the position of the United States courts on the political exception. To qualify as a political offence 'the crime must be incidental to and form a part of political disturbances. It must be in furtherance of one side or another of a bona fide struggle for political power'.[1]

(After a lapse of twenty-five years Artukovic, then aged 84, was arrested in California in November 1984 on a new extradition warrant from Yugoslavia. The case is still before the United States courts.)

The 1959 Artukovic judgement was reinforced in the same year in the case of *Ramos v. Diaz* in Florida. The new revolutionary government of Fidel Castro in Cuba had sought the extradition of two members of its rebel army who had been convicted of killing a prisoner whom they mistook for a supporter of the ousted Batista regime. The prisoner had in fact been a prominent member of the Cuban Communist party which was allied with the new government.

The two Cubans, who had escaped and fled to the United States, claimed their offence was political. The Florida court agreed, noting that the killing took place in the 'early days of victory' of the Cuban revolution and so was 'part of a political uprising and disturbance'.[2] Subsequent cases pulled back a little from the extraordinarily wide-ranging immunity conferred in *Karadzole v. Artukovic*, but held firmly to the position that offences would be regarded as political if there

was a widespread political disturbance and they were incidental to it.

When the Nationalist revolt broke out anew in the North
of Ireland in 1969-70 there was widespread sympathy from
Irish Americans and vociferous support from some. The
United States became an important source of funds and
weapons for the Provisional IRA and men and women on the
run once again made their way across the Atlantic.

The British government put considerable pressure on its
United States ally to clamp down on Irish Republican
activities and gradually the administration responded. The
authorities acted against gun-running, illegal anyway under
United States law, and more controversially, refused visas to
Irish Republican activisits. At length, in May 1978, Peter
Gabriel McMullen was arrested in California on a British
extradition warrant.

McMullen was a 30 year old former soldier in the British
army's crack parachute regiment, who came originally from
Co. Derry in the North of Ireland. He was stationed at Holywood Barracks outside Belfast at the time of Bloody Sunday
in January 1972 when units of his regiment fired into a
crowd of unarmed protesters in Derry city, killing 13 of
them. McMullen was outraged. He planted a bomb in the
barracks and deserted.

He joined the IRA and was actively involved with them
until 1974 and intermittently thereafter. In 1976 he was
arrested in the Republic and jailed for IRA membership. In
April 1978 he entered the United States on a false passport
and was arrested a month later. The British authorities sought
his extradition on a charge of planting a bomb at a military
barracks at Claro in Yorkshire in 1974. McMullen admitted
the offence but claimed it was political, saying he had been
an active member of the IRA at the time.

It was the first time since *Lynchehaun*'s case in 1903 that
a United States court had been asked to rule on Irish political
violence. Magistrate Frederick J. Woelflen gave his judgement
in May 1979. He based his ruling on the Castioni and

Artukovic cases, saying:

> The standards that must be established to bring what
> otherwise would be common law crime (e.g. murder)
> within the political offence exception . . . are two-fold.
> One, the act must have occurred during an uprising and
> the accused must be a member of the group participating
> in the uprising. Second, the accused must be a person
> engaged in acts of political violence with a political
> end . . . Even though the offence be deplorable and hein-
> ous the criminal actor will be excluded from deportation
> if the crime is committed under these prerequisites.[3]

The magistrate noted that Britain had derogated from international conventions because of the 'emergency' situation in
the North of Ireland. And he said: 'We cannot shut our eyes
to what has occurred in Northern Ireland since 1970 through
1979 with respect to the activities of the PIRA in its insurgent and terrorist activities . . .'

All this led to 'the obvious inescapable conclusion that an
insurrection and a disruptive uprising of a political nature did
in fact exist in Northern Ireland in 1970 and particularly in
1974 when Mr McMullen is charged with the crimes against
Claro Barracks . . .' Magistrate Woelflen held that the bombing was incidental to the uprising, that McMullen was a member of the uprising group and that his motives were political.
He dismissed the extradition application.

The McMullen judgement relied on the very broad interpretation of a political offence adopted in *Karadzole v. Artukovic*. But early in 1981 that interpretation was narrowed
sharply by the United States Court of Appeals in *Eain v.
Wilkes*.[4] Ziad Abu Eain was a young Palestinian from
Ramallah in the Israeli-occupied West Bank area. He was
arrested in Chicago in August 1979 two months after arriving
in the United States. Israel sought his extradition on a charge
of planting a no-warning bomb at a youth rally in Tiberias in
May 1979. Two schoolboys were killed and 36 others

injured.

Abu Eain admitted he was a member of the Palestine Liberation Organisation, but denied planting the bomb. In any case he pleaded that it was a political offence. The court rejected the plea, arguing that there was no clear connection between the random bombing of civilians and overthrowing the Israeli government:

> This definition of 'political disturbance', with its focus on organised forms of aggression such as war, rebellion or revolution, is aimed at acts that disrupt the political structure of a State and not the social structure . . . The exception does not make a random bombing intended to result in the cold-blooded murder of civilians incidental to a purpose of toppling a government, absent a direct link between the perpetrator, a political organisation's political goals, and the specific act . . . Otherwise, isolated acts of social violence undertaken for personal reasons would be protected simply because they occurred during a time of political upheaval . . .

The court also showed signs of a more direct political concern of its own, saying the political exception 'should be applied with great care lest our country become a social jungle and an encouragement to terrorists everywhere'.

Abu Eain was extradited to Israel in December 1981 and convicted after a controversial trial where major discrepancies emerged in the prosecution case. He was given a life sentence, though 18 months later he came tantalisingly close to release. In November 1983 the International Red Cross arranged an exchange of 4,380 Palestinians held by the Israelis for six Israeli soldiers held by the PLO in Lebanon. Ziad Abu Eain was on the list of prisoners to be exchanged and was actually taken to an Israeli airport with the others, ready to fly to Algeria, when Israeli officials suddenly took him back to prison.

In May 1985 there was another smaller exchange, 1,150

Palestinians for three Israelis. The Palestinians insisted that Abu Eain be included and this time there was no hitch. He was released. The Israelis, who had sought his extradition on the grounds that the offence involved was not political, had by implication acknowledged that he was a political prisoner.

Would the Abu Eain case change the United States courts' attitude to Irish cases? It did not take long to find out. Desmond Mackin, a 25 year old Belfast man, had been arrested in New York in October 1980. Britain was seeking his extradition on a charge of attempted murder of an undercover British soldier in the Andersonstown area of Belfast in March 1978. He had absconded while on bail in Belfast.

Mackin came from a Republican background. His grandfather had been active in the IRA in Co. Fermanagh in the 1920s and his grandmother had been a member of Cumann na mBan, the women's section of the IRA. Two of his uncles had been jailed in the North during the 1950s IRA campaign. His family had been burned out of their home by a Loyalist mob in 1969 and he had joined the IRA.

Mackin had been jailed in the North for IRA membership from 1972 to 1976. When he got out of jail he was again involved with the IRA and also became Belfast organiser for Sinn Fein, its political wing. He was well known to the RUC and British army. On 18 March 1978 a group of plain clothes soldiers appear to have been shadowing Mackin and another suspected IRA man Robert Gamble in Andersonstown. The British authorities alleged Mackin fired at the soldiers. In the ensuing melée Mackin and Gamble and one of the soldiers were wounded.

Mackin pleaded the political exception. Magistrate Naomi Reice Buchwald gave her judgement on 31 August 1981.[5] She was very thorough. Her judgement ran to 101 pages. Unlike McMullen, Mackin denied the actual charges so there was a 'probable cause' hearing to begin with, i.e. a hearing to determine if there was a *prima facie* case against him — the United States law requires the establishment of probable cause before there can be any extradition.

Magistrate Buchwald held there was not sufficient evidence on the attempted murder charge, but there was a case to answer for possessing and firing a weapon. There was another preliminary issue. The United States administration, under the newly-elected President Reagan, was unhappy about the courts' refusal to extradite McMullen, which had not improved relations with its closest ally, Mrs Thatcher. It was worried that future extradition decisions could annoy other allies.

The administration submitted to the court that the executive, not the courts, should make decisions on the political exception. Magistrate Buchwald firmly rejected the idea, pointing out that in 'more than 80 years of jurisprudential history' the political offence issue had always been decided by the courts.

She went on to review the case law on extradition from *In re Castioni* and *Re Ezeta* to the McMullen and Abu Eain cases. From it she distilled three basic criteria by which to determine if the offence was political:

1. Whether there was a war, rebellion, revolution or political uprising at the time and site of the commission of the offence;
2. Whether Mackin was a member of the uprising group;
3. Whether the offence was 'incidental to' and 'in furtherance of' the political uprising.

The criteria were very similar to those adopted by the McMullen court. She rejected a government argument that the *Eain v. Wilkes* judgement indicated that irregular or guerrilla organisations like the PLO or the IRA did not qualify for the political exception. She held that the only relevance of the Eain judgement was to rule out acts 'of an anarchistic nature, directed at the civilian population'. That did not arise in Mackin's case.

Having reviewed Irish history from the 1920s on and

especially after 1968 Magistrate Buchwald concluded that 'there was a political conflict in Andersonstown, Belfast, Northern Ireland, in March 1978 which was part of an on-going political uprising, fluctuating in intensity, but never-theless of sufficient severity' to satisfy the first of the three criteria.

The uprising group was the Provisional IRA and Mackin was clearly a member of it. As for the third criterion, the magistrate held that 'unlike . . . an instance of random terror-ism directed at the civilian population, Mackin's act was aim-ed directly at a member of the British army . . . In short it was a confrontation between "two parties in the State as to which is to have the government in its hands".'

Mackin was discharged. The Court of Appeals upheld the judgement in December 1981. But Mackin had entered the United States illegally and the Immigration and Naturalisation Service had begun deportation proceedings against him. He agreed to be sent to the Republic of Ireland — like most Northerners he was entitled to Irish citizenship. He was deported to Dublin on 31 December 1981. No attempt has been made to extradite him from the Republic or to prosecute him under the Criminal Law Jurisdiction Act. His companion in the Andersonstown incident in 1978, Robert Gamble, who had faced similar charges, was acquitted by a Belfast court.

The United States authorities did not discourage easily. One month after Magistrate Buchwald dismissed the application to extradite Mackin, a third IRA man was arrest-ed in California. The British government wanted William Joseph (Liam) Quinn to face charges of murdering a London policeman, sending letter bombs to prominent British figures and conspiring to cause explosions in London. The case would again test whether the Eain judgement would alter the courts' attitude to Irish cases.

Quinn was actually a United States citizen, born of Irish American parents and brought up in California. He became interested in the Northern conflict, resigned his job and went to Ireland in September 1971 to join the IRA. They sent him to join an active service unit in London and the British authorities claimed he was associated with a group later called the Balcombe Street Four. They had carried out a long list of bombings in England until they were finally captured after a siege at a house in Balcombe Street in London in December 1975.

Quinn himself had returned to Ireland earlier in 1975 and had been jailed for a year on a charge of IRA membership. He went back to the United States in 1978 and no action was taken against him until 1981. He was now accused of conspiring in 1974-5 with the Balcombe Street Four to plant a number of bombs and to send letter bombs to Sir Max Aitken, chairman of the *Daily Express* newspaper, Bishop Gerard Tickle, Catholic chaplain to the British army and Crown Court Judge John Buzzard. Quinn was also accused of murdering Police Constable Stephen Tibble while evading arrest in London in February 1975. He pleaded that these were political offences carried out as part of an IRA campaign in Britain.

At the lower court level the Eain judgement, with its narrower definition of a political offence, did affect the case. A local magistrate rejected Quinn's plea in September 1982. But the case was reviewed by Judge Robert P. Aguilar in the District Court for Northern California. He gave his judgement in October 1983.[6] The United States government had again argued that decisions on the political exception should be left to the executive. Judge Aguilar noted that the administration had been trying for some time to get Congress to agree to that. He made a ringing defence of the role of the courts.

Leaving decisions on the political exception to the courts ensured that they were not swayed by

> political considerations such as the favour due or not due to the country seeking extradition, or the sympathy to the political position of the person whose extradition is

sought. Until Congress decides that such political considerations should be part of the determination . . . the
judiciary must guardedly preserve its role in making un-
biased and independent decisions on the applicability
of the . . . exception.

The magistrate had adopted the three criteria for determining a political offence that had been specified in the Mackin
case — a political uprising, membership of the uprising group,
and an offence that was incidental to the uprising. He had
accepted that 'a state of severe violent political unrest existed
in the United Kingdom, including Great Britain' at the time
of the offences, but relying on the *Eain v. Wilkes* judgement,
he held that the bombings alleged against Quinn were not
sufficiently clearly connected with this unrest because they
were directed against civilians. He also held there was not
enough evidence to prove Quinn was a member of the uprising group.

Judge Aguilar reaffirmed the broad view of the political
offence. He rejected the idea that it was necessary to prove
membership of the uprising group, arguing that such a requirement could infringe the accused's protection against self-
incrimination under the Fifth Amendment. Anyway, he said,
there was ample proof that Quinn was a member of the IRA.
As for the offences being connected with the uprising, he
pointed out that the bombing involved in the Eain case was
directed against Jewish civilians totally at random, whereas
'the three letter bombs attributed to [Quinn] were not
directed at the general civilian population, but to a bishop
to the British military and to two other representatives of the
British establishment'. They were part of a plan to 'bring the
British to the bargaining table with the PIRA'.

The judge also criticised the tone and implications of the
Eain decision, warning that it could lead to the courts taking
sides in the conflicts which gave rise to extradition hearings:

The court's emotion in dealing with the case is reflected

in its discussion regarding terrorists who commit barbarous acts and its conclusion that the political offence exception 'should be applied with great care lest our country become a social jungle and an encouragement to terrorists everywhere'. Such expressions of emotion have not been part of the historic function of the extradition court while determining the applicability of the political offence exception . . .

Liberal application of the Eain decision could result in the extradition court making judgements as to the goals of a particular uprising group and the appropriateness of the acts of the uprising group. Inherent in any situation where political change is sought are conflicting opinions on the merits of the sought-after change and the methods being used to seek the change. Extradition courts must avoid becoming caught up in such controversy.

Judge Aguilar noted that 'bombing incidents by those opposed to British rule are the historical form of violent expression in the long controversy over such rule [in Ireland]'. He held that the bombings in this case were 'incidental to' and occurred 'in the course of' the political uprising. As for the shooting of PC Tibble, Judge Aguilar ruled that it occurred during an attempt to evade an arrest which would lead to the discovery of an IRA bomb factory nearby. He held that it too was sufficiently connected with the political uprising to qualify as a political offence. He dismissed the extradition application.

The Quinn judgement was doubly embarrassing for the United States administration. It did not help relations with the British government which was particularly sensitive about bombings in London and attacks on British police or members of the British establishment. It did not look well when the Reagan government was advocating a world wide campaign against terrorism — though not of course against the activities of groups which it supported, like the Contras in Nicaragua, the guerrillas in Afghanistan and the Khmer

Rouge and their allies in Kampuchea.

The United States government appealed the Quinn decision to the Court of Appeals for the Ninth Circuit. No decision has yet been given and in the meantime Quinn has been in jail continuously since September 1981, the equivalent of a substantial prison sentence. The authorities have also used other methods to try to get rid of Irish and other political fugitives. The Immigration and Naturalisation Service (INS) has pursued Peter McMullen, trying to get him deported for entering the United States illegally, even though McMullen has broken with the IRA and has appeared on several television programmes denouncing them.

McMullen claimed, with some justification, that his life might be in danger from the IRA if he was deported even to the Republic and an immigration court initially accepted his plea. The INS repeatedly appealed the case and in May 1984 got an order against McMullen. He counter appealed and the case has not been finally resolved.

The INS also succeeded in the summer of 1984 in deporting Michael O'Rourke, an IRA man who had been convicted of explosives offences in the Republic and escaped from jail and made his way to the United States in 1978. There was no extradition arrangement between the Republic and the United States at the time so deportation was the only avenue open to the administration. O'Rourke spent nearly five years in jail in the United States awaiting a final decision.

The INS did not of course confine itself to Irish cases. In the early 1980s it was responsible for the deportation of large numbers of political fugitives from Latin America as well. Some of them faced the likelihood of assassination by death squads on their return.

Meanwhile the Reagan administration also supported a number of Bills before Congress which, like the European Anti-Terrorist Convention, would have excluded most acts of violence from the category of political offences, or which would have transferred decisions on political extradition from the courts to the executive. There was resistance to the

Bills, however, and they lapsed with the elections in November 1984.

In the meantime, in three major cases, the United States courts had reasserted their independence, reaffirmed the traditional doctrine of the political exception to extradition and confirmed that in their view the activities of the IRA in Northern Ireland and Britain fell firmly within the definition of political offences which were exempt from extradition.

8: 'The Judicial Authorities have been Rendered Obsolete'

At 7.00 a.m. on the morning of St Patrick's Day 1984 Dominic McGlinchey and three other men were captured by gardaí in a house in Co. Clare after a short gun-battle. Eighteen hours later McGlinchey was handed over to the RUC on the Border between Newry and Dundalk. He was the first Republican activist to be extradited since the Southern state was set up in 1922.

The decision had been coming for some time. Despite the passing of the Criminal Law Jurisdiction Act, the Northern authorities had continued to issue extradition warrants for Republican fugitives. The procedure for dealing with them had become pretty standardised. The district court would order the suspect's extradition. He or she would appeal to the High Court on the grounds that it was a political offence. Where it was obviously connected with the IRA or the INLA — a new and smaller splinter group — the state rarely contested the claim and extradition was refused.

The definition of a political offence had become fairly wide. In July 1978 Francis Heron who was wanted for beating up a woman in Strabane, Co. Tyrone, claimed that it was a punishment beating ordered by the IRA and so was a political offence. Counsel for the state commented that it was 'an unconventional form of political activity' but did not contest the issue. The High Court refused to extradite him.

As late as February 1981 the High Court was still applying the political exception as before. In that month it released Martin O'Hanlon who was wanted for conspiracy to cause explosions in Belfast in 1976. O'Hanlon had said he had been a member of the IRA 'engaged in an armed struggle against the RUC and the British army'.

But the political pressure for extradition from Britain and from Unionist politicians had continued. And the composition and attitudes of the Republic's Supreme Court had been changing.

From 1961 to 1973 the Supreme Court, led by Chief Justice Cearbhall Ó Dálaigh, ably supported by Mr Justice Brian Walsh, had played an active liberalising role, stressing those sections of the Constitution which guaranteed the rights of the individual and curbing the arbitrary exercise of power by the executive. It was Ó Dálaigh and Walsh who had struck down the old Backing of Warrants procedure between the Republic and Britain in 1964 and who had so firmly asserted the political offence exception to extradition in *Bourke*'s case and in *Magee v. O'Rourke* in 1970.

But Ó Dálaigh had joined the European Court in 1973 — and became President of the Republic in 1975. He was succeeded as Chief Justice by W. O'B. FitzGerald and then by Tom O'Higgins, who held the position from late 1974 to the beginning of 1985. Both were conservative men and there were strong suggestions they were appointed to try to curb the liberalising zeal of the Supreme Court, especially at a time when Dublin governments had begun to introduce harsh measures to deal with the overspill of the Northern 'Troubles' into the South.

O'Higgins was a former Fine Gael Cabinet Minister and Presidential candidate and his family background was strongly anti-IRA. His grandfather had been killed by the IRA during the Civil War, his uncle had been Minister for Home Affairs during the Civil War and was assassinated by Republicans in 1927. His father had been a founder of the quasi-fascist Blueshirt organisation in the 1930s and he himself had been associated with it as a student. He was followed onto the Supreme Court by a number of other more conservative judges.

The court did not change overnight — Mr Justice Walsh led

the Irish delegation on the post-Sunningdale Law Enforcement Commission in 1974 and the High Court continued
throughout the 1970s to follow the precedent of the *Bourke*
judgement in extradition cases. But gradually the court's
rulings became more conservative on a whole range of issues.

Then in July 1981, a Fine Gael-Labour Coalition government returned to power. Relations between the outgoing
Fianna Fáil government and Britain had reached rock-bottom
following the British government's hard line attitude towards
a hunger-strike by Republican prisoners in the North. The
new government seemed anxious to win favour with the
British Prime Minister, Mrs Thatcher. The Attorney-General,
Peter Sutherland, let it be known that he favoured extradition of Republican prisoners.

In October 1981 an extradition case involving a political
offence claim came before the Supreme Court, the first since
Magee v. O'Rourke in 1970. The British police were seeking
the extradition of Longford man Maurice Hanlon on a charge
of handling stolen explosives in London in 1971. The case
had been heard by Mr Justice Doyle in the High Court in
1974, but he had not given a decision until October 1980,
following an extraordinary delay.

Hanlon had claimed the explosives were for the use of the
IRA but produced no evidence to back his claim. He had a
long string of convictions for breaking and entering and even
for receiving stolen chickens. The High Court had rejected his
plea. In the Supreme Court Mr Justice Seamus Henchy,
supported by the Chief Justice and Mr Justice Frank Griffin,
agreed with the High Court judgement that 'there was no
acceptable evidence . . . that any of the proceeds of [the
accused's] criminal activities was used for the purposes of the
IRA'.[1]

That was enough to dismiss the appeal, but he went on to
add that 'even if it had been found as a fact that the explos-
ive material . . . had been intended for transmission to the
IRA, it would not necessarily follow that the accused would
be exempt from extradition on the ground that the charged

offence is a political offence or an offence connected with
a political offence. There has been no decision of this court
on such a point. It must be left open for an appropriate case.'

There had in fact been a decision on that or a similar point
in *The State (Magee) v. O'Rourke*, but it was clear the court
was about to change its attitude to IRA-related offences and
was only waiting for the opportunity. The opportunity came
in Dominic McGlinchey's case.

Dominic McGlinchey grew up with the Northern Troubles.
Born in South Derry, he was 14 when the Civil Rights movement began. He joined the IRA in 1971 at the age of 17 and
was interned without trial for a year shortly afterwards. A
year later he was jailed for 18 months for possessing firearms.
Three of his brothers have also been jailed for IRA offences.

From 1974 to 1977 McGlinchey was active in the South
Derry unit of the IRA led by Francis Hughes who died on
hunger-strike in 1981. It was one of the most active IRA
units, carrying out a large number of attacks on the RUC,
UDR and British army. At one stage the RUC issued 'wanted'
posters and leaflets with photographs of McGlinchey, Hughes
and a third man, Ian Milne. In September 1977 McGlinchey
was arrested in the Republic and jailed for possessing firearms and resisting arrest. While in jail he changed his allegiance
from the IRA to the INLA.

In January 1982 he was released from Portlaoise prison
and arrested on a warrant seeking his extradition to the North
on a charge of murdering 67 year old Mrs Hester McMullan
near Toomebridge, Co. Antrim. One of Mrs McMullan's sons
was a member of the RUC Reserve and her daughter worked
for the RUC. She was killed in March 1977 when a group of
armed men shot and wounded her son and then opened fire
on the house as well. The IRA claimed responsibility for the
attack. The extradition application did not refer to the
wounding of Mrs McMullan's son or to the family's connections with the RUC.

McGlinchey claimed it was a political offence or an
offence connected with a political offence and said he

believed that if he was extradited, he would be charged with
other offences which were political. He did not admit involvement in the murder of Mrs McMullan and at his eventual trial
in the North strongly denied it. There was of course no
requirement under the Extradition Act for the Northern
authorities to establish a *prima facie* case against him.

The case came before the High Court in May 1982. The
pressure for extradition was increasing. A month earlier the
conference of the Association of Garda Sergeants and Inspec-
tors in the Republic had called for extradition of members of
paramilitary groups. Mr Justice Gannon rejected McGlinchey's
plea, saying there was nothing in his affidavit to show that
the killing of Mrs McMullan was connected with a political
offence. McGlinchey appealed to the Supreme Court.

In the meantime, in July 1982, the European Parliament
had passed a motion calling on member states to extradite
'terrorists', following a debate in which British and Northern
Unionist MEPs had criticised the Irish government's refusal
to extradite.

McGlinchey abandoned the plea that Mrs McMullan's
death was connected with a political offence and concentrated on the point that he might be charged with other
offences that were political. He tried to submit an extra affidavit with new information that statements made to the RUC
by a number of IRA members in South Derry had implicated
him in the killing of a UDR man in his native village of
Bellaghy in March 1977. The court refused to accept the affidavit.

Chief Justice Tom O'Higgins gave his judgement on 7 December 1982, supported by Justices Henchy and Griffin, the
same judges who had already signalled a change in the court's
attitude to political offences in *Hanlon v. Fleming* in 1981.
The McMullan murder charge was no longer at issue but the
Chief Justice evidently wanted to use the occasion to spell
out the court's new position. He specifically rejected the legal
precedents on which his predecessor Cearbhall Ó Dálaigh had
based his opinions and outlined a new and somewhat bewil-

dering test for political offences.

Having stressed Mrs McMullan's age and sex, he said:

> . . . [It] should not be deduced that if the victim were
> someone other than a civilian who was killed or injured as
> a result of violent criminal conduct chosen in lieu of what
> would fall directly or indirectly within the ordinary scope
> of political activity, the offence would necessarily be
> classified as a political offence . . . The judicial authorities
> on the scope of such offences have in many respects been
> rendered obsolete by the fact that modern terrorist viol-
> ence . . . is often the antithesis of what could reasonably
> be regarded as political . . .

Then came the new test. Each case would have to be
judged according to its particular circumstances and whether
they showed that 'the person charged was at the relevant
time engaged in what reasonable, civilised people would regard as political activity'. The Chief Justice did not define
whom he would regard as 'reasonable, civilised people'.

The court rejected McGlinchey's plea that he might be
charged with other, clearly political, offences and in a con-
cluding passage the Chief Justice appeared to exclude all
actions involving violence from the category of political
offences:

> This court is invited to assume that because of the exist-
> ence of widespread violence organised by paramilitary
> groups in Northern Ireland, any charge associated with
> terrorist activity should be regarded as a charge in res-
> pect of a political offence or an offence connected with
> a political offence. I am not prepared to make any such
> assumptions.
>
> The excusing *per se* of murder and of offences
> involving violence and the infliction of human suffering,
> done by, or at the behest of, self-ordained arbiters, is the
> very antithesis of the ordinances of Christianity and civil-

isation and of the basic requirements of political activity.[2]

It was a remarkable decision which effectively overturned the judicial practice of the previous ten years. It was welcomed by the incoming Coalition government which had just defeated a short-lived Fianna Fáil administration. Attorney-General Peter Sutherland hailed it as a landmark, saying it distinguished between political activity and 'terrorist activity' and put the emphasis on the nature of the crime rather than its motive. He spelled out its implications more sharply than the Chief Justice had done: 'Even if a person committed an offence against a member of the security forces in Northern Ireland he could no longer be shielded from extradition by claiming a political motive.'[3]

The significance of the McGlinchey judgement passed the general public by because McGlinchey himself had absconded during the Supreme Court hearing and so there was no dramatic handover at the Border — yet.

McGlinchey went on the run and became the reputed head of the INLA, achieving a quite remarkable notoriety. The press dubbed him the most wanted man in Ireland and he was blamed for virtually every violent incident which happened in the Republic over the next 18 months. He gave an interview to the *Sunday Tribune* newspaper in November 1983 and claimed he had killed 30 people and taken part in over 200 bombings and shootings since 1972. But he denied involvement in the McMullan killing.

When McGlinchey was caught in Clare on St Patrick's morning 1984 the government and the Supreme Court seemed extraordinarily anxious to deliver him to the RUC. The government, pressed by Attorney-General Sutherland, decided the extradition order should be implemented immediately — apparently against the advice of the Director of Public Prosecutions who thought he should be charged with offences arising from the shoot-out in Co. Clare. The three men captured with him were convicted and given jail terms a few months later.

McGlinchey's lawyers obtained an injunction that afternoon from the High Court to delay the extradition for a few days so they could challenge its validity. The Supreme Court held an unprecedented late night bank holiday sitting to overturn the injunction and McGlinchey was sped on his way that very night. Once again the judges were Chief Justice O'Higgins and Justices Henchy and Griffin.

The RUC were not slow to follow up the McGlinchey decision. Two months later they issued a warrant for Philip McMahon on a charge of escaping from custody in March 1975. McMahon had fled South after escaping and had been jailed there for a year in October 1975 so they had known where to find him, but had not thought it worthwhile issuing a warrant. Now they evidently felt they might have more success. Supreme Court Justice Niall McCarthy commented in a later case (*Shannon v. Fanning*): 'It was abundantly clear that the issue of [McMahon's] warrant flowed directly from the decision in McGlinchey's case.'

The McMahon case was to underline, in an embarrassing way, the extent to which the Supreme Court had overturned the precedents on political offences. McMahon had been jailed in the North for an armed robbery carried out by the IRA. He and a number of others had tried to escape from Long Kesh prison camp but were caught. They were charged with attempting to escape and were brought to Newry courthouse for trial in March 1975, whereupon 12 of them did escape.

When McMahon was arrested in the South he pleaded that it was a political offence. He had escaped 'for the purpose of regaining my liberty and continuing the struggle for the liberation of the six counties of Northern Ireland from British rule.' He said he had subsequently left the IRA. Mr Justice Ronan Keane rejected McMahon's plea in the High Court in August 1983, basing his decision on the McGlinchey judgement.

But there was an awkward aspect to the case which Mr Justice Keane had brushed aside. Four of McMahon's fellow escapers had been caught in the South not long after the event. They had pleaded that the escape was a political offence and the High Court had agreed. The state had not challenged the decision.

McMahon appealed to the Supreme Court which gave its decision in June 1984. Applying the logic of the McGlinchey decision, it should probably have rejected his plea, but the Chief Justice did not go into the details of the offence. He said if McMahon was extradited 'it would mean that contradictory declarations in relation to the same incident would have issued from our courts. If such occurred, respect for the administration of justice in our courts would surely suffer and the courts' process would certainly have been abused.' He allowed the appeal.[4]

McMahon's case was merely an embarrassing reminder of a previous policy. The court soon reverted to its new line, unconcerned about whether it contradicted previous decisions.

Seamus Shannon, a Tyrone man living in the South, had been arrested in July 1983 on an extradition warrant charging him with the murder of 84 year old Sir Norman Stronge and his son James in January 1981.

Sir Norman and his son were landowners at Tynan, Co. Armagh, close to the border with Co. Monaghan. Sir Norman had been a Unionist MP in the Northern parliament for 31 years and was Speaker of that body until he retired in 1969. He was head of the Royal Black Institution, a brother organisation of the Orange Order, and was the Queen's Deputy Lieutenant for Co. Armagh, a ceremonial post. James Stronge had succeeded his father as local Unionist MP and later was a member of the Northern Assembly. He was also a member of the RUC Reserve.

A group of IRA men had burst into the Stronges' home at Tynan Abbey in January 1981, shot the two men dead and set fire to the house. The IRA claimed it was a reprisal for the killing of a number of Republican activists by Loyalist groups and for an assassination attempt on former Mid-

Ulster MP Bernadette McAliskey and her husband a fortnight previously.

Seamus Shannon denied any involvement in the Stronge murder, but claimed it was a political offence. Once again the Northern authorities did not have to establish a *prima facie* case. Mr Justice McWilliam rejected his plea in the High Court in January 1984 saying: 'I consider I am bound by the views of the Supreme Court [in the McGlinchey case]. . .'

The Supreme Court gave its judgement on 31 July 1984.[5] The Chief Justice was supported again by Justices Henchy and Griffin. This time he went a little further in overturning historical precedents. He explicitly rejected 'the "political incidence theory" . . . which found expression in a number of English cases dating from *In Re Castioni* right up to recent times, requiring for recognition as a political offence merely that the offence be committed during and as part of a political disturbance.' He held instead that the Oireachtas had left it to the courts to decide 'on the particular facts and circumstances of each case, viewed in the light of the standards and values which obtain in this country at the particular time.' He did not indicate, however, how changing standards and values were to be measured.

Chief Justice O'Higgins accepted that the Stronges had been killed by the IRA, whose objectives included 'the reunification and the reintegration of the national territory'. But he referred back to his McGlinchey judgement with its apparent exclusion of all forms of violence from the political exception and its new criterion — what 'reasonable civilised people would regard as political activity'.

He rejected Shannon's appeal saying: 'Apart from the fact that . . . the Provisional IRA have abjured normal political activity in favour of violence and terrorism, the circumstances disclosed as to the murders in question here were so brutal, cowardly and callous that it would be a distortion of language if they were to be accorded the status of political offences or offences connected with political offences.' This was another departure from the Castioni judgement, where

Justice Sir Henry Hawkins had held that the court could not judge the morality of individual actions which were in furtherance of an overall political uprising.

The Chief Justice also rejected Shannon's claim that he might be charged with other offences, saying — though it is not so specified in the Extradition Act — that 'extradition proceeds on the assumption that the rule of specialty will operate.'

Two other members of the five-man court gave separate opinions. (Extradition cases could be heard by a three member court as McGlinchey's had been, but all subsequent cases have been heard by five judges.)

Both said Shannon should be extradited, but they were evidently unhappy with the arguments of the Chief Justice. Mr Justice Anthony Hederman, a former Fianna Fáil Attorney-General, explicitly rejected the 'reasonable civilised people' test:

> In my view such a test, even if it could be considered in the present case, could only create uncertainty . . . A great many things which undoubtedly constitute political activity would not be regarded by most people as either reasonable or even civilised activity, but that would not necessarily detract from the character of the offence. The overthrow of the Government of a State by armed force with the object of replacing it by another Government might very well be regarded by a great number of people as being neither reasonable nor civilised but nevertheless it is a classic example of the political offence. The murder or the attempted murder of the tyrannical or despotic rulers of a State with the object of replacing them by a democratic Government would be regarded as political activity though repugnant to many people who would regard any activity involving violence as being unreasonable and uncivilised . . .

Mr Justice Hederman also acknowledged that the IRA was

involved in a struggle for political objectives:

> For many years the Provisional IRA in Northern Ireland
> have been endeavouring by force of arms to expel the
> British administration and its armed forces for the avow-
> ed purpose of reuniting Northern Ireland with the rest of
> the island to the exclusion of the Government of the
> United Kingdom. It is common knowledge that there is
> an armed conflict in progress for many years in Northern
> Ireland between the Provisional IRA and the defence
> forces and the security forces of the United Kingdom.
> They in turn respond by employing counter-insurgency
> methods and tactics . . .

He went so far as to assume 'for the purpose of this case'
that actions 'done in the course of and in furtherance of the
stated objectives' would be 'relative political offences'. But
then he drew a rather fine distinction. Noting that the IRA
had claimed the Stronge killings were 'reprisals for hardships
or injustices alleged to have been inflicted upon members of
the Nationalist population of Northern Ireland', he held that
there was no evidence that they were part of 'the armed
struggle to eject the British'.

More crucially, he also said that 'the decisive criterion to
determine whether an ordinary criminal offence becomes a
relative political offence is whether the perpetrator acted
with a political motive or for a political purpose.' Since
Shannon denied any involvement in the offence the court
could not determine his motives and so could not allow his
appeal.

This 'subjective' approach, focusing on the offender's
motive, was in complete opposition to the Chief Justice's
'objective' approach which concentrated on the nature of the
offence. It also created its own problems. It put a totally
innocent person at a major disadvantage since he or she could
not give evidence about their motivation for something they
had not done. It could force a guilty party to incriminate

him or herself, providing material for a prosecution under the Criminal Law Jurisdiction Act or that could be used in an eventual trial if the person was extradited — as was to happen in Dominic McGlinchey's case. Ironically Mr Justice Hederman had argued just that point as counsel for Mrs Roisín McLaughlin in her appeal against extradition ten years earlier.

The final judgement was by Mr Justice Niall McCarthy. He flatly rejected Justice Hederman's view that 'in order to assess motive, the individual charged must admit his involvement in the crime'. He avoided direct comment on the McGlinchey judgement but set out a different set of criteria for determining political offences, criteria which included both 'subjective' and 'objective' factors. They were:

1. The true motivation of the individual or individuals committing the offence . . .
2. The true nature of the offence itself.
3. The identity of the victim or victims.
In assessing all or any of these factors, the proximity of each factor to the alleged political aim is critically important and is capable of objective assessment.

He accepted that the Stronge killings 'were, in the minds of those involved, in intended furtherance of their declared aim of the reunification and reintegration of the national territory.' But he held that the connection between them and the political objective was not sufficiently close to qualify for the political exception.

The Supreme Court showed the same urgency in handing over Shannon as they had with McGlinchey. Shannon had also challenged the constitutionality of Part III of the Extradition Act but the court simply announced it had rejected his arguments and would give its reasons later. He was not brought to court to hear the final judgement in his political offence plea but was simply taken from Portlaoise prison and driven to the Border a few hours later. The court gave its detailed judgement on his constitutional action in November

1984, four months after he had been handed over to the Northern authorities.

Following Shannon's case the legal position on extradition for political offences was highly confused. The Chief Justice had jettisoned the legal precedents and introduced a new test which even one of his colleagues said 'could only create uncertainty'. Justices Hederman and McCarthy agreed that the IRA's motives were political and seemed to agree that violent acts could be regarded as political offences, but they disagreed over whether the plaintiff would have to admit the offence in order to plead that it was political.

The one thing they all seemed to agree on was that the plaintiffs should be extradited.

9: 'A Patently Unconstitutional Construction . . .'

The Supreme Court in the Republic not only extradited Dominic McGlinchey to the North, it also played a key role in convicting him there. McGlinchey was not brought to trial until December 1984, nine months after he had been handed over to the RUC. When the case went to court it emerged that a crucial part of the evidence against him consisted of two affidavits he had submitted while fighting extradition in the South — one of them had not even been allowed in evidence by the Supreme Court.

Chief Justice O'Higgins and President of the High Court Thomas Finlay had authorised the release of the affidavits to the RUC without consulting McGlinchey or his lawyers and without any public notice or hearing. It was an unprecedented and disturbing development. In his attempts to resist extradition McGlinchey had been obliged to admit to membership of the IRA and involvement in armed attacks in the North, but he had not been warned that his admissions could be used against him in the Northern courts if he was extradited. That seemed to undermine one of the fundamental principles of the common law — that defendants must not be obliged to incriminate themselves.

Moreover, the affidavits did not exist when McGlinchey's extradition was first applied for, so an important part of the case against him was only assembled after extradition proceedings had begun.

McGlinchey was tried before Judge Hutton in Belfast Crown Court. The only direct evidence linking him with the killing of Mrs McMullan was two finger prints found on a window of the getaway car used by the IRA unit which attacked her house. Finger prints found on a moveable object like a car are notoriously inconclusive by themselves. McGlinchey, who denied any part in the killing, claimed in an unsworn statement that he had been given a lift in the car a few days before the shooting and his finger prints could have been placed there innocently.

The prosecution reinforced the finger print evidence by using McGlinchey's affidavits to establish that he was a member of an IRA active service unit in the area at the time. They cited forensic evidence to show that all four guns used in the attack on Mrs McMullan and her son had been used in other IRA attacks in the area at the time McGlinchey was active.

It was a tenuous argument but Judge Hutton accepted it. The Republic's Supreme Court had emphatically rejected the suggestion that Mrs McMullan's murder was a political offence or connected with a political offence. Ironically Judge Hutton based his findings on the belief that it was an IRA attack, motivated by the McMullan family's connection with the RUC: 'I am satisfied that the McMullan family were attacked by a gang of Republican terrorists because their son was an RUC reservist and their daughter worked at an RUC station.' He was also satisfied that the guns had been used in other Republican attacks on the North's security forces. As for the finger prints, he said: 'It would be a coincidence beyond the realms of all reasonable possibility if the finger prints had been put on the car on some occasion other than when the terrorist gang were making their getaway in the car.'[1]

He held that McGlinchey was a member of the attacking group and convicted him of murder. He sentenced McGlinchey to life imprisonment, but said that since he did not know his exact role in the killing, it would be unfair to recommend a minimum term in jail. McGlinchey has appealed.

The McGlinchey verdict probably came as a relief to the authorities in the South. There had been growing concern about the long delay in bringing him to trial and suspicion that it was because the RUC were casting about for evidence to bolster their case. A South Derry man already serving a fifteen year jail sentence for the manslaughter of Mrs McMullan had claimed in July 1984 that RUC detectives had offered him inducements similar to those offered to 'supergrass' witnesses to give evidence against McGlinchey in the murder trial. The prisoner refused.[2]

But if McGlinchey's conviction was a relief to the Southern courts and authorities there was another aspect of the case which was embarrassing. During the trial evidence almost identical to that in relation to the McMullan killing had been produced against McGlinchey in relation to an IRA attack on the RUC station in the nearby village of Ahoghill in Co. Antrim in June 1977, in which three RUC members were wounded. McGlinchey's finger prints and those of his close associate Francis Hughes were found on the van used in the attack.

No attempt had been made to have McGlinchey extradited to face charges in connection with the Ahoghill attack. The suspicion inevitably arose that the RUC had chosen to press the McMullan case rather than the Ahoghill one because the Southern courts were more likely to break with tradition in a case involving the killing of a civilian woman than in one involving an attack on a fortified police station. Once the warrant was issued for the McMullan killing the Northern authorities had no wish to cloud the issue and draw attention to McGlinchey's other IRA activities.

That suspicion was strengthened in February 1985 when two men were tried in Belfast for involvement in the killing of an RUC man in Cookstown, Co. Tyrone — not far from McGlinchey's home area — in May 1983. The court was told that five finger prints made by McGlinchey were found on a map in a van used by the INLA unit involved and two more were found in a house used as a hide-out by the group. One of the accused gave evidence that McGlinchey had led the group and had forced him (the accused) to ferry them away across Lough Neagh. The two were convicted in March 1985. One was jailed for life and the other for ten years.[3]

This killing took place after the Supreme Court had ordered McGlinchey's extradition in December 1982, and while he
was on the run, but before he was eventually handed over.
The RUC could have issued a further extradition request for
him on this charge, but did not do so. Again it looked as if
they did not want to queer the pitch by drawing attention to
his involvement in attacks on the Northern security forces.

Some extraordinary sidelights were cast on the McGlinchey case — and perhaps on other cases — when Chief Justice
Tom O'Higgins gave lengthy press and radio interviews on his
retirement in January 1985. He said Mrs McMullan had been
alone in her house with an infant when she was shot, and that
she was shot with an Armalite rifle.[4] According to the evidence
at McGlinchey's trial three weeks earlier, Mrs McMullan's husband and grown-up daughter were in the house with her and
there was no infant. Nor was she killed by an Armalite rifle.
In fact no Armalite was fired at the house.

The former Chief Justice also stated quite incorrectly that
Nicky Kelly, the central figure in another legal *cause celebre*,
had never protested his innocence. Such inaccuracy about the
details of major cases, in one of which he had given a headline-
making judgement, did not increase confidence in the decisions of the courts.

Mr O'Higgins confirmed that he had been concerned about
the delay in bringing McGlinchey to trial and said that if
McGlinchey had been charged with anything other than the
McMullan murder, he would have advised the Taoiseach to
change the extradition law.

But he seemed to recognise and regard as acceptable that
the RUC had only put together their case against McGlinchey
after he was extradited: '. . . I should imagine what happened
was that they may have felt that McGlinchey was the man
they wanted. They probably hadn't, when they applied initially, the evidence or the evidence that they had may have
gone out of date.'

A whiff of embarrassment over developments in the
McGlinchey case — which became clear at a preliminary in-

quiry in September 1984 — did not prevent the Supreme
Court from reaffirming its new line on the political offence
exception two months later and in the process giving a remarkable endorsement to the Northern security and judicial
systems.

Seamus Shannon had challenged the constitutionality of
Part III of the Extradition Act as well as pleading that the
murder of Sir Norman and James Stronge was a political
offence. As we have seen, the Supreme Court rejected the
challenge in July 1984 without giving its reasons. Eventually it got round to giving them on 16 November 1984,
nearly four months later.

Some of the points raised by Shannon's lawyers were fairly technical but three of them raised broader issues. They
argued that 'the law, procedure and practice relating to the
interrogation, detention and trial of persons accused of
politically related or terrorist offences in Northern Ireland
fall considerably short of the minimum requirements for
criminal trials in this State.'

They claimed that the absence from Part III of the Act —
dealing with Britain and the North — of a clause prohibiting
extradition where the plaintiff's position might be prejudiced
'on account of his race, religion, nationality, or political
opinion' was contrary to a generally recognised principle of
international law. There was a clause to that effect in Part II
of the Act and in the European Convention on Extradition
on which it was modelled.

They argued that the fact that there was no obligation on
the courts to establish that there was a *prima facie* case
against the extraditee was also in conflict with international
law and failed to protect the rights of the citizen, contrary to
Article 40 of the Constitution.

The President of the High Court, Mr Justice Finlay, had
rejected these claims in May 1984, giving the Northern system a clean bill of health. He declared:

There is no evidence that any person suspected of or

charged with such terrorist type crime has been prejudiced by reason of his race, religion, nationality or political
opinion. I must, therefore, conclude on the evidence
before me that persons being dealt with by the security
and judicial authorities in Northern Ireland . . . [for]
terrorist offences are equally dealt with irrespective of
the question of their race, religion, nationality or political
opinion.[5]

As for the claim that law enforcement practice fell below
the requirements in the Republic, he said: 'I find this assertion totally unwarranted by the evidence before me.' And he
held that the fact that there was no obligation to establish
a *prima facie* case did not infringe the extraditee's constitutional rights.

In the interim there was a public outcry about the failure
of the Northern courts to convict RUC men accused of murdering unarmed IRA and INLA members and the Taoiseach,
the Minister of Foreign Affairs, and the leader of the Opposition, Mr Haughey, all expressed concern about both the
RUC and the Northern courts.

But when in November Mr Justice Seamus Henchy came to
outline the reasons for the Supreme Court's rejection of
Shannon's claim he completely endorsed Mr Justice Finlay's
judgement. On the question of the law and practice in the
North, he said Mr Justice Finlay's 'careful elaboration and
analysis of the evidence' withstood all criticism.[6]

On the question of the possibility of the plaintiff's position being prejudiced on account of his/her race, religion,
nationality or political opinion, Mr Justice Henchy said:
'There is no evidence in this case to justify a conclusion that
there are grounds (not to speak of *substantial* grounds) for believing that the . . . [plaintiff's] position may be prejudiced
for any of those reasons.'

He dismissed the *prima facie* argument by saying that
extradition agreements operated 'on the assumption that
both parties . . . will act in good faith.' There was a hint of

unease about the McGlinchey case, however, when he added that if 'it were to transpire that the charge in the warrant was trumped up or insubstantial, or brought for ulterior purposes, the good faith which is a prerequisite for the operation of extradition would be absent and the extradition arrangements would break down.'

Ironically, just as the Republic's courts were copper-fastening their move away from the political offence exception and their closer alignment with the Northern system, a United States court refused to extradite an IRA man who had been convicted of murdering a British army officer in Belfast.

Joe Doherty was one of four IRA men who took over a house on Belfast's Antrim Road in May 1980. They were armed with a US-made M60 heavy machine gun and were planning to ambush a British army patrol. Instead a plain clothes unit of the British army's undercover SAS regiment surprised them. After a shoot-out in which the leader of the SAS team, Captain Herbert Westmacott, was killed, Doherty and his companions surrendered.

Doherty was convicted of murder by a Belfast court in June 1981, but escaped from the city's Crumlin Road prison before sentence. He was sentenced to life imprisonment in his absence. He made his way to the United States and was arrested in New York in June 1983. The British authorities sought his extradition for the murder conviction and for escaping from jail.

The case was heard by Judge John Sprizzo in the district court for the southern district of New York. The United States and British authorities took it very seriously. A State Department official warned the court that 'the application of the political offence doctrine to deny extradition could cause damage in relations between Great Britain and the United States', and that the damage 'would not necessarily be limited to Great Britain, but could extend to other countries with strong national policies against terrorism.'

The court became a miniature Irish forum as the United States Attorney called an Assistant Chief Constable of the RUC, an official of the British Home Office and Unionist politician Robert McCartney as pro-extradition witnesses. Judge Sprizzo got a crash course in Irish history as Seán MacBride SC, former Mid-Ulster MP Bernadette McAliskey and *Irish Press* editor Tim Pat Coogan gave evidence for Doherty.

The judge gave his decision in December 1984. He was influenced by the *Eain v. Wilkes* judgement and the trend in Britain and much of Western Europe to cut back the political exception and reserve it almost exclusively for non-violent offences. He adopted more stringent criteria for a political offence than in the previous Irish cases, saying not every act 'committed for a political purpose or during a political disturbance' should be regarded as a political offence.[7]

No act should be regarded as political 'where the nature of the act is such as to be violative of international law, and inconsistent with international standards of civilised conduct.' War crimes and actions directed specifically against civilians were out. But Judge Sprizzo did not accept many of the restrictions suggested by the United States Attorney's office:

> The court rejects the notion that the political offence exception is limited to actual armed insurrections or more traditional and overt military hostilities . . . recent history demonstrate[s] that political struggles have been commenced and effectively carried out by armed guerrillas long before they were able to mount armies in the field. It is not for the courts . . . to regard as dispositive [i.e. warranting dismissal] factors such as the likelihood that a politically dissident group will succeed, or the ability of that group to effect changes in the government by means other than violence, although concededly such factors may at times be relevant . . .
>
> Nor is the fact that violence is used in itself dispositive. Instead the court must assess the nature of the act, the

context in which it is committed, the status of the party committing the act, the nature of the organisation on whose behalf it is committed, and the particularised circumstances of the place where the act takes place.

Using these criteria, Judge Sprizzo held that Doherty's offences 'present the assertion of the political offence exception in its most classic form.' This was not a case of 'a bomb . . . detonated in a department store, public tavern or a resort hotel, causing indiscriminate personal injury, death and property damage.' Nor was it an attack on 'civilian representatives of the government, where defining the limits of the political offence exception would be far less clear.' It was a straightforward clash with the British army.

The judge was not anxious to extend the protection of the political exception to 'every fanatic group', so the court had to look at the nature and structure of the organisation involved. But he held that the Provisional IRA 'has both an organisation, discipline and command structure that distinguishes it from more amorphous groups such as the Black Liberation Army [in the United States] or the Red Brigade.'

There was some slight consolation for the British government in the case. Judge Sprizzo rejected suggestions that the non-jury Diplock courts in the North were unfair. 'The Court concludes that both Unionists and Republicans who commit offences of a political character can and do receive fair and impartial justice . . .' But that endorsement was qualified by a footnote drawing attention to the fact that cases were referred to the Diplock courts 'on the basis of a determination that what would otherwise be common law offences are politically motivated'.

Doherty's extradition was refused.

The United States government then filed an unprecedented motion asking another judge of the same court to review Judge Sprizzo's decision on the grounds that it was 'erroneous . . . arbitrary, capricious and an abuse of discretion.' The government's motion was dismissed 'with prejudice' in June 1985. In the meantime Doherty remained in jail awaiting the outcome of deportation proceedings by the United States Immigration and Naturalisation Service.

The Doherty decision annoyed the British government and the Reagan administration, anxious to show its opposition to 'terrorism' against its closest ally. At the end of June 1985 the two governments signed an agreement to amend the 1972 Anglo-American extradition treaty to exclude acts of violence from the category of political offences. The amendment which would be retrospective, will have to be ratified by the United States Senate.

Also towards the end of 1984 the scope of the whole extradition issue in Ireland was widened by the adoption of new extradition agreements with the United States and Australia — the Republic already had agreements with about seventeen countries which were parties to the European Convention on Extradition. The United States agreement took the form of a treaty which had been signed in July 1983 and came into operation in November 1984. Unusually for a bilateral treaty, it contained unequal obligations on the question of the establishment of a *prima facie* case or 'probable cause' as a condition of extradition. If the Republic sought the extradition of someone from the United States, it would have to show 'reasonable grounds for believing that an offence has been committed and that the person sought committed it.' There was no such obligation on the United States.

The treaty was retrospective and half a dozen fugitives from the United States were quickly arrested in Ireland but none of them pleaded the political exception.

The Australian agreement was more controversial. On 25 October 1984 Robert Trimbole, who was wanted in Australia on charges of drug trafficking and murder, was arrested in Dublin. The Republic had no extradition agreement with Australia but a reciprocal arrangement was hastily concluded on 26 October. In the meantime Trimbole was held under the Republic's 'anti-terrorist' Offences Against the State Act.

When the extradition agreement came into effect he was re-arrested in accordance with it.

In February 1985 the High Court held that this 'was a gross misuse of Section 39 [of the Offences Against the State Act] which amounted to a conscious and deliberate violation of [Trimbole's] constitutional rights.' It held that there was no justification for arresting Trimbole under the Offences Against the State Act and that it was just a ruse to hold him. Mr Justice Seamus Egan held that this illegality tainted Trimbole's subsequent detention under the Extradition Act and ordered his discharge.[8] The Supreme Court later upheld his judgement.

But neither the Doherty decision nor the extension of the extradition machinery to other continents caused any re-think by the Irish Supreme Court on political offences.

In January 1985 Chief Justice Tom O'Higgins had resigned to become a member of the European Court in Luxembourg. He was succeeded as Chief Justice by the former President of the High Court, Thomas Finlay. There was considerable interest to see whether the Supreme Court would stick to the tough line on extradition which had been so closely associated with O'Higgins and with the Attorney-General, Peter Sutherland, who had also gone to Europe — as the Republic's member of the EEC Commission.

There was not long to wait. At the end of February 1985 the court heard an appeal against extradition by John Patrick Quinn, a 38 year old man from Ballina, Co. Mayo. Quinn was wanted for obtaining £600 from a London bank on false pretences by passing stolen travellers' cheques. He had appealed on the grounds that he was a member of the INLA at the time, and the offence and others on the same day, involving another £9,000, were committed to raise funds for the INLA.

The High Court had rejected Quinn's appeal simply on the grounds that he had not established sufficient connection between passing the cheques and a political offence. The Supreme Court took a very different line. The new Chief Justice, supported again by Justices Henchy and Griffin, focused on a statement in Quinn's affidavit that the aims of the INLA were 'the establishment of a 32-county workers' Republic by force of arms and *inter alia* a military campaign against the forces of the Crown within the six counties of Northern Ireland and the United Kingdom and elsewhere'.

Chief Justice Finlay noted that all laws in the Republic had to conform to the Constitution. He then declared that the objective of the INLA as outlined

> necessarily and inevitably involves the destruction and setting aside of the Constitution by means expressly or impliedly prohibited by it, cf. Articles 15.6 and 39. To interpret the words 'political offence' . . . so as to grant immunity or protection to a person charged with an offence directly intended to further that objective would be to give to the section [of the Extradition Act] a patently unconstitutional construction. This court can not, it seems to me, interpret an Act of the Oireachtas as having the intention to grant immunity from extradition to a person charged with an offence, the admitted purpose of which is to further or facilitate the overthrow by violence of the Constitution and of the organs of State established thereby.[9]

Justices Hederman and McCarthy in separate judgements adopted the same position.

It was an astonishing judgement in a number of ways. It was not at all clear, without a good deal more argument, that the INLA's objective did *necessarily* involve the forcible overthrow of the Constitution. It was at least arguable that its objective actually involved the fulfilment of the Constitution by extending its effectiveness over the whole of the national territory. As for the 'workers' Republic' part, that might well involve changing the Constitution but it did not follow that that could only be done by force of arms.

There was as much — or as little — real evidence that the IRA sought to overthrow the Republic's Constitution by force as there was that the INLA did. On this reasoning it seemed the court would also hold that no action carried out on behalf of the IRA could be regarded as political.

For Chief Justice Finlay himself it seemed an extraordinary about turn from his previous decisions — notably in the Fr Bartholomew Burns case in 1974 when he said quite firmly that 'it seems to me that the safe-keeping of explosives for an organisation attempting to overthrow the state by violence is according to that test an offence of a political character'.

The decision seemed to indicate as well that the then Supreme Court had been wrong to refuse the extradition of George Magee in *Magee v. O'Rourke* in 1970. To the lay person it seemed extraordinary that the Supreme Court could have heard four or five extradition cases involving self-confessed members of 'subversive' organisations over the previous three years and the High Court could have heard anything up to 100 cases over 10 years without anyone adverting to this fundamental Constitutional point.

If the court sticks to this line it seems extradition will become automatic for members of Republican paramilitary groups. Successive governments — most notably Liam Cosgrave's at the time of the Sunningdale conference — will have been wrong about extradition and so will the Irish delegation on the 1974 Law Enforcement Commission. The 1976 Criminal Law Jurisdiction Act will have been totally unnecessary and so will the government's refusal to sign the European Convention on the Suppression of Terrorism.

Such a total reversal of policy amounts effectively to changing the law, and changing it on the basis of a controversial and distinctly arguable interpretation of the objectives of the IRA and INLA. Such a decision would seem to be the prerogative of the Oireachtas rather than the courts. The Oireachtas might be more influenced by a commodity mentioned by Chief Justice Finlay in his judgement in *Bartholomew Burns v. the Attorney-General* — common sense.

Refusing to extradite Fr Burns for storing explosives for the IRA, Mr Justice Finlay said:

[I]f it were required to aid that legal decision with a
common sense appraisal of what the meaning of political
offence were, it would be difficult to avoid the same
conclusion. In ordinary parlance and use of words, the
phrases, an offence committed with a political motive,
persons carrying out certain activities for political ends,
have become as common as the day is long, and by that
test, which is not the necessary or binding test as far as I
am concerned, it seems to me that in the narrow sense in
which I am asked to decide it, the offence charged is a
political one.

In the common view as well it looked distinctly as if the
Supreme Court had decided by 1982 that members of the
IRA or INLA accused of crimes in the North or Britain
should be extradited, and had since then been casting about
for arguments to justify its action.

Not all members of the judiciary appeared to agree with
the Supreme Court, however. In June 1985 in the High Court
Mr Justice Seamus Egan refused to extradite Clareman
Gerard Maguire to England on a robbery charge when
Maguire claimed it was carried out on behalf of the IRA.
Noting that Maguire's affidavit said nothing about overthrowing the Constitution, Mr Justice Egan said he was not
prepared to hold that offences committed by the IRA
could never be regarded as political 'until the Supreme Court
tells me [so] specifically.'[10]

As for John Patrick Quinn, the case against him was dismissed by a London magistrate when the papers had not been
prepared by the police by June 1985, three months after his
extradition. The Supreme Court had delivered its weightiest
judgement yet in the case of a man who never even came to
trial. A requirement to establish probable cause before extradition cases could go ahead might have saved the court a lot
of embarrassment.

Conclusion

In November 1982 a Dublin-born Columban missionary in the Philippines, Fr Niall O'Brien, was charged with the murder of a local town mayor on the island of Negros. The mayor had been killed by the Communist New People's Army fighting against the regime of President Ferdinand Marcos.

Fr O'Brien spent months in custody during which he won the sympathy of most Irish people. Eventually he was cleared of the charge. But if Fr O'Brien had returned home at the end of 1982 and the Philippines government had sought his extradition, what would have happened?

The murder of the mayor was obviously political, but Chief Justice O'Higgins' judgement in the McGlinchey case appeared to exclude all acts of violence from the political offence exception. He spelled that out more clearly in his interview with the *Sunday Press* when he retired. 'We just said murder is not a political offence . . . violence and brutal offences of one kind or another are so serious that their criminality exceeds their political aspect.'[1]

Neither could Fr O'Brien have avoided extradition by showing that the charge was trumped up. Though Part II of the Extradition Act allows the government of the Republic to specify that a state requesting extradition must show that there is a *prima facie* case against the accused, none of the agreements actually negotiated with other countries includes such a requirement.

So Fr Niall O'Brien should have been extradited. As it happens the Republic has no extradition agreement with the

Philippines, but then an agreement was made almost overnight with Australia in October 1984 when the Australian
government sought the extradition of Robert Trimbole.

The hypothetical O'Brien case illustrates just how much
the Supreme Court's recent judgements have undermined
the principle of non-extradition for political offences. That
principle has played an important part in struggles for
political freedom in many countries over the years, not least
in Ireland. Under it Spanish Republicans found shelter from
Franco in Paris, Algerian exiles in Egypt and Tunisia, Zim-
babweans in Tanzania.

It is still very important today. Political exiles from El Salvador and Guatemala find refuge in Nicaragua and Mexico,
African National Congress and SWAPO members shelter in
other African states, Iranian exiles go to Paris, Tamils from
Sri Lanka flee to India. Not many political refugees have
found their way to Ireland — a few Chileans after the overthrow of President Allende, a few Vietnamese boat people —
but if fugitives from some of the above conflicts arrived here
and their extradition was sought by the governments they
opposed, few people would believe they should be handed
over, even if they had been involved in acts of violence. Yet
as the law now stands they would be extradited.

Chief Justice O'Higgins justified his reversal of precedent
in the McGlinchey case by saying that the judicial authorities
had been rendered largely obsolete by 'modern terrorist violence' which was 'often the antithesis of what could reason-
ably be regarded as political'. That was very much the reasoning behind the European Convention on the Suppression of
Terrorism (1977).

It is questionable whether the upsurge of urban guerrilla
violence in Europe in the 1970s was different in kind from
previous decades. Zionist groups in Palestine — the Irgun and
the Stern Gang, EOKA in Cyprus, the FLN in Algeria — all
used 'terrorist' methods and were just as blood-thirsty as the
1970s groups. What was different was the advent of television,
which brought the effects of bombings and shootings into

everyone's living room, and the fact that the attacks were directed against West European governments themselves or were on their soil.

The new trend in Europe to virtually eliminate the political offence exception smacked of panic and of what John A. Costello warned against in 1955 when he told the Dáil that 'international law is not a mutual insurance system for the preservation of established governments.'

There was another more important difference between the headline grabbing 'terrorism' of the 1970s and that of the 1940s, 1950s and 1960s, but it was rarely referred to at the time. It was the nature of the groups and the conflicts involved. The West German Red Army Fraction, the Red Brigades in Italy, the Angry Brigade in Britain were miniscule groups, isolated from any significant section of society, fighting an almost private war of their own. They were quite unlike EOKA or the FLN, national liberation movements firmly rooted in their communities, or even the more complicated cases of the Zionists in Palestine. It was a distinction United States Judge John Sprizzo drew in the case of Joe Doherty in December 1984 when he contrasted the IRA with the Red Brigades and the Black Liberation Army and refused to extradite Doherty.

This 'new terrorism' was not beyond the scope of the established judicial authorities at all. It was quite like the anarchist violence dealt with in the Meunier case in Britain as early as 1894. The 'new terrorism' could have been dealt with without overturning precedents or altering the law and thereby threatening the principle of the political exception.

(This is not necessarily to advocate the extradition of members of these groupuscules There is another principle involved as well, that of fair trial and humane treatment. The draconian measures adopted by, for example, West Germany, to crush the Red Army Fraction and its treatment of 'subversive' prisoners raise serious questions about whether fugitives should be extradited there for politically motivated crimes.)

'Traditional' political violence continued alongside the 'new terrorism' in Europe in the 1970s and France at least acknowledged the difference. While the French authorities extradited a number of Red Army Fraction members to West Germany, they refused to extradite Basque guerrillas to Spain, acknowledging that the Basque conflict had deep historical roots and the campaign of violence by ETA had considerable popular support.

President Mitterrand's government eventually did extradite some ETA militants in September 1984, when Spain had acquired a socialist government, a regional assembly had been set up in the Basque country, and ETA's military campaign had lost much of its support. But the French authorities quickly thought better of it and resumed a policy of deporting ETA members to Latin American or West African countries instead.

To the outside observer there can be little doubt into which category of political violence the Provisional IRA fall. The grievances which motivate them — Partition and the treatment of the Catholic minority within Northern Ireland — are as old as the Northern state itself. The minority as a whole has never accepted the Northern state and a section of it has turned to political violence in every generation. The present-day IRA is no miniscule faction, they have substantial popular support, demonstrated by the approximately 40% of the Nationalist population which voted for the IRA's political wing, Sinn Féin, in elections in 1983, 1984 and 1985.

Nor are the Provisional IRA's methods substantially different from those of their predecessors, the IRA of 1919-22 — especially the units which fought in the North at the time. The 'Old IRA' killed off-duty policemen, burned down commercial property and tossed grenades into shipyard trams. Their successors just have greater fire-power and modern explosives.

With the perspective conferred by distance and non-involvement, Judge John Sprizzo in New York had no difficulty categorising the situation. The IRA's campaign was 'but the latest chapters in the unending epic' of the Anglo-Irish conflict and a shoot-out between the IRA and British soldiers was 'the assertion of the political offence exception in its most classic form.'

The principle of non-extradition of political offenders is a valuable safeguard for those struggling for political change, against repressive regimes, for the rights of minorities and for oppressed peoples and nationalities. It often does not suit great powers or economically powerful countries with overseas interests to protect. It is important that small neutral states like the Republic of Ireland, without vested interests, defend that principle and do not lightly abandon it because of a mood of panic in some of its European neighbours or because of political pressure from its nearest neighbour.

But if the Republic is to adhere to the principle of non-extradition it cannot logically exclude crimes of violence and it cannot deny that the IRA's activities in the North exactly fit the definition of political offences. (The same reasoning would apply to the INLA, even though it is much smaller and has little direct political support. Most members of the Northern minority would make little practical distinction between the INLA and IRA and the political support for Sinn Féin would indicate some level of support or tolerance for the INLA as well.)

Perhaps not all the activities of the IRA and INLA would qualify for the political exception. Derogations from the general principle have been made by most countries, including the Republic, in the case of war crimes, genocide and aircraft hijacking. The common thread seems to be an attempt to protect uninvolved citizens. So if it could be established that an IRA action was deliberately aimed at uninvolved civilians it might not warrant protection, though if there was any doubt it should favour the fugitive.

If the Republic's courts were to uphold the political exception but rule out actions aimed at uninvolved civilians,

however, there would be a strong temptation to the RUC
to press such charges against someone whom they really
wanted for straight political offences — as it was widely
believed they did in the McGlinchey case. The best safeguard against that would be insistence on the establishing of
a *prima facie* case before extradition was granted.

The *prima facie* issue is extremely important in its own
right. Extradition for any offences is a serious question. It
involves the removal of a fugitive from one jurisdiction to
another, and almost certainly a period in custody there.
It should never be undertaken without due cause shown and
especially not in politically-related cases. It is all very well
for the Supreme Court to talk of a presumption of good
faith on the part of the requesting state (*Shannon v. Ireland and the Attorney-General*). But as Judge Sprizzo
pointed out in *In re Doherty* in the United States: '[I]t is
certainly at least arguable that the United Kingdom may
not be entirely neutral with respect to the issue of Irish
independence because it is the end of British rule in Ireland
that has been and continues to be the principal objective of
the Irish Republican movement.'

To presume total good faith and disinterestedness on the
part of the Northern or British law enforcement systems
towards members of the IRA is distinctly naive. Do the
Republic's courts have the right to be so trusting at the ex-
pense of the people who appear before them? The evidence
of selectivity in deciding which charges to prefer against
McGlinchey and the way in which the case against him was
assembled *after* he was handed over do not encourage such
a presumption of good faith.

Even accepting that the IRA's activities in the North —
or in Britain where they have also carried their campaign for
British withdrawal from the North — qualify for the political exception, what of the argument used by the Supreme
Court in *Quinn v. Wren*? That the objective of the INLA,
and impliedly the IRA, is to overthrow the Constitution by
force of arms and so the activities of those organisations

cannot be protected by courts established under the Constitution.

There is no evidence to sustain that view. Since the end of the Civil War in May 1923 no faction of the IRA has attempted any sort of armed campaign against the government of the Free State or the Republic. Following a series of gunfights between IRA men and special branch detectives in the South in the 1939-45 period the IRA formally announced in 1949 that in future no aggressive action would be taken against the security forces in the South.

Since the present Northern Troubles began that seems to have been modified and there have been a number of shootouts between gardaí and Irish army soldiers and IRA members, but they have all been in the course of robberies or escapes. There have been no indications that they or even the more trigger happy INLA are out to overthrow by force the institutions of the State. However criminal their conduct in the Republic in the eyes of the courts, that does not justify saying it is something which it quite evidently is not.

There is another important aspect of the extradition issue. The British and American common law traditionally applied the political exception if they were satisfied simply that there was a serious political conflict going on at the time and the offence was part and parcel of it. The continental European tradition stressed as well the question of whether the extraditee would get a fair trial.

The Irish Extradition Act reflects both traditions. Part II which covers all other countries includes the clause prohibiting extradition if there are substantial grounds for believing that the extraditee's position might be prejudiced 'on account of his race, religion, nationality or political opinion.' Part III covering the United Kingdom leaves out that clause. There is no justification for having less safeguards in regard to extradition to the North or Britain than for other countries. On the contrary, there is every reason to be more concerned about the fate of prisoners in politically related cases in the North or Britain.

The Supreme Court held in *Shannon v. Ireland and the Attorney-General* that there was no evidence to justify a conclusion that Shannon's position might be prejudiced in the North. Dog does not eat dog perhaps, particularly in adjoining jurisdictions, but the court seems to have taken a very narrow view of even the evidence before it.

Calling in aid that other quality cited by Chief Justice Finlay in *Bartholomew Burns v. Attorney-General* [1974] — common sense — the view must be rather different. Since 1968 the Northern law enforcement system has repeatedly been indicted by outside agencies. The European Commission on Human Rights in 1976 found the Northern authorities guilty of torture of a number of detainees subjected to 'interrogation in depth' in 1971-2 when internment was introduced. The European Court later reduced the finding to one of 'inhuman and degrading treatment', but even that was damning enough.[2]

In 1978 an Amnesty International mission to the North held that 'maltreatment of suspected terrorists by the RUC has taken place with sufficient frequency [in the previous 2-3 years] to warrant the establishment of a public inquiry to investigate it.'[3] A subsequent British government-appointed inquiry under Judge Bennett found that 'a number of persons received injuries which were not self-inflicted and were sustained during the period of detention at a police office.'[4]

Suspects were being beaten to obtain confessions which were then used to secure convictions in special non-jury courts. The beatings largely ceased after the Bennett Report but were replaced as a method of securing convictions by 'supergrasses' — acknowledged members of paramilitary groups who were offered immunity or inducements to incriminate their colleagues. The supergrass cases did much to taint the whole system in the North. Dáil Éireann passed a resolution in December 1984 declaring that the reliance on supergrass evidence was damaging the North's legal and judicial system.

The report of the New Ireland Forum, representing the three main parties in the South and the constitutional Nationalist SDLP in the North, noted that 'extraordinary security actions have taken place [in the North] that call into question the effectiveness of the normal safeguards of the legal process.'[5]

Public unease about the Northern system in the South and among Northern Nationalists reached a peak in the summer of 1984 after Northern courts had acquitted a number of RUC men of murdering five unarmed members of the IRA and INLA in two separate and highly controversial incidents. One of the North's senior judges, Lord Justice Gibson, actually commended three RUC men for 'their courage and determination in bringing the three deceased men . . . to the final court of justice.' In another case Lord Justice Mac-Dermott commended another RUC man on his marksmanship.[6]

Reflecting this unease, even spokesmen for the extremely anti-IRA government of the Republic have recently taken quite a different line from the Supreme Court on the acceptability of the legal system in the North. The Minister for Foreign Affairs, Peter Barry said in August 1984 . . . 'the Nationalist population does not believe that the system of justice is in their interest or is for their benefit. They don't believe that and I am afraid there have been examples which gave them cause for that belief.'[7]

The Taoiseach Dr FitzGerald said on British television in September 1984 that the RUC was 'completely unacceptable' as a police force. He said: 'There is more recent and very serious alienation from the institutions of justice. Judges have expressed themselves in terms no member of the minority could accept as reflecting justice.'[8]

There is certainly little public confidence in the Republic that Nationalists accused of politically-related offences would get a fair trial in the North and would be treated equally with a member of the security forces accused of serious crime. The acquittal of the RUC men in the 'shootto-kill' cases, against what seemed to lay people to be the trend of the evidence, contrasted with the conviction of Dominic McGlinchey on what seemed to the lay person quite tenuous evidence. Some Southern lawyers have queried whether the Republic's non-jury Special Criminal Court would have convicted McGlinchey on the evidence presented against him.

Where serious doubts exist about the likelihood of fair trial they must strongly reinforce the case against extradition for political offences. Even in a case where the political exception did not apply — like a deliberate attack on civilians — but where there were obvious political connections, doubts about fair trial should give the courts pause before they order extradition. The extraditee should be given the benefit of any doubt.

Much the same reasoning applies to the courts and the law enforcement system in Britain. Irish people feel that the British police, or at any rate the 'anti-terrorist' units are biased against them. The harsh Prevention of Terrorism Act is used almost exclusively against the Irish and there is considerable unease about the convictions of a number of Irish people charged with bombing offences in England. The most dubious convictions were those of the Maguire family and Guiseppe Conlon for allegedly possessing explosives in London; of Conlon's son, Gerard, and others for bombing a pub in Guildford; and of six men for the Birmingham pub bombings in November 1974.

All have repeatedly proclaimed their innocence and a group of acknowledged IRA bombers have claimed responsibility for the Guildford bombing. The British authorities have rejected all calls for an inquiry into these cases and many people would doubt that Irish prisoners would get a completely impartial trial in England.

Would Dominic McGlinchey and Seamus Shannon have been extradited if the law had been interpreted as I have suggested?

Had there been a *prima facie* inquiry the extradition applications might have fallen at the first hurdle. McGlinchey's affidavits which were a key part of the evidence at his trial did not exist when the application was filed. Shannon has not yet been tried but the only real evidence against him is also a fingerprint on a getaway car.

McGlinchey having conceded that the murder of Mrs McMullan could not be regarded as political, the Supreme Court refused to hear additional evidence that he might be charged with another offence which was political.

It is a moot point. There is ample proof now that the RUC had as much, or more, evidence against him on 'political' charges as on the McMullan charge. They did not charge him with these, but there is still no certainty that they would not do so were he to be acquitted of the McMullan charge on appeal. There is no rule of specialty to prevent them doing so. Then there is the question of fair trial. It emerged after McGlinchey's extradition that a controversial RUC operation, which resulted in the death of two INLA members in Armagh in December 1982, had been intended for McGlinchey. Would he have been killed as well if he had turned up? Could he be expected to get a fair trial from a system where many believe the RUC had set out to assassinate him?

All in all I think a refusal to extradite McGlinchey would have been more in keeping with the tradition of the political exception. And besides, he had charges to answer in the South as well.

In Seamus Shannon's case, however unsavoury the murder of an 84 year old man, there can be no doubt that it was politically motivated and that Sir Norman Strange and his son were attacked as members of the Unionist political establishment in the North. The Old IRA had carried out similar political killings in their time notably those of Unionist MPs William Twaddell and Sir Henry Wilson in May and June 1922. The political exception indicates no approval of the actions involved, merely a recognition that they are part of a real political conflict.

McGlinchey and Shannon were difficult cases and ones unlikely to evoke much public sympathy — they may well
have been chosen for precisely that reason. In cases of
attacks on serving members of the security forces in the
North there should be no doubt at all. To use the term Chief
Justice O'Higgins used in Shannon's case, it would be 'a
distortion of language' to claim that they were not political
offences.

There is a third important aspect of the extradition
question — the Northern Ireland problem and how to solve
it. Does extraditing political offenders (for, legal niceties
aside, everyone knows that that is what they are) help or
hinder a solution to the Northern problem? The answer inevitably depends on what is seen as the origin of the problem.

The New Ireland Forum put it succinctly:

> Since 1922 the identity of the Nationalist section of the
> community in the North has been effectively disregarded
> . . . they have had virtually no involvement in decision-
> making at the political level. For over 50 years they
> lived under a system of exclusively Unionist power and
> privilege and suffered systematic discrimination. They
> were deprived of the means of social and economic
> development, experienced high levels of emigration and
> have always been subject to high rates of unemployment.

Attempts to redress these grievances by non-violent means
at the end of the 1960s 'were met with violence and repression' and 'the conditions were thus created for the revival
of a hitherto dormant IRA which sought to pose as the
defenders of the Nationalist people.'

Job discrimination had continued and security policies
'have, since 1974, deepened the sense of alienation of the
Nationalist population.' The Forum Report warned that by
1984 things were getting steadily worse and 'constitutional
politics' were now on trial.

The Dublin government had traditionally been seen as

'the second guarantor' of the Nationalist minority in the North — and Jack Lynch, Taoiseach at the beginning of the Troubles, had confirmed that view. A contributory factor to the current level of alienation has been the belief that Dublin governments abandoned that role during the 1970s. For the Dublin authorities now to extradite people whom most Northern Nationalists (including many SDLP supporters) regard as political offenders, handing them over to courts where Nationalists do not believe they will get a fair trial, is to make members of the minority community feel even more isolated and betrayed.

To continue to extradite political offenders to the North would be to deepen that alienation of the Northern minority which the Dublin government has pledged itself to end.

The Ulster Unionists and the British government have put intense pressure on Dublin on the issue, but giving in to it is likely to be counter-productive. The Forum Report argued cogently that a whole series of repressive measures in the North 'were introduced on the basis that they were essential to defeat terrorism and violent subversion, but they have failed to address the causes of violence and have often produced further violence.'

The whole thrust of the Forum's argument was that there is no military solution to the Northern problem and the attempt to impose one only exacerbates the problem. The IRA are an expression of a revolt by Northern Nationalists. They will not go away until the conditions that produced them go away. To step up co-operation in the British security drive would be to encourage the British government in the disastrous belief that they can either win a military victory or reduce things to a level of violence acceptable to Britain, but totally unacceptable to the people of Ireland, North or South. Irish governments should, on the contrary, spare no effort to convince Britain that the problem will never be resolved until they tackle its root cause, partition and the position of the minority in the North.

For three reasons then — to uphold an important principle

of international law; because of a lack of confidence in the impartiality and standards of the Northern law enforcement system; and in order to break with the British policy of pursuing an illusory military victory in the North — the Republic should return to a policy of refusing to extradite people accused of political offences in connection with the Northern conflict.

The Extradition Act should be amended to require evidence that a *prima facie* case exists before anyone is extradited, and the clause prohibiting extradition where an extraditee's position might be prejudiced on account of his/her race, nationality, religion or politics should be added to the section dealing with Britain and the North, together with a rule of specialty. The Oireachtas should spell out that it wants the political exception retained with its traditional meaning and that it should apply to offences arising out of the Northern conflict. If the courts continue to erode the whole principle of the political exception the Minister for Justice should exercise the power reserved to him under the Act and refuse to extradite political offenders.

The Criminal Law Jurisdiction Act (1976) would then remain and alleged offenders in the North and Britain could be tried under it. I believe two of the three arguments against extradition apply to the 1976 Act as well — that political offenders from another jurisdiction, where there is a serious political conflict going on, should not be pursued and that the Republic should not get caught up in Britain's security policy in the North. Besides, the British side have never taken the Act seriously. It is a left-over from the Sunningdale agreement which the British themselves allowed to collapse. I think it should be abandoned, like the rest of the agreement. But that is an argument for another day.

Footnotes

CHAPTER ONE

1 ní Chinneide, Síle, *Napper Tandy and the European Crises of 1798-1803*, National University of Ireland, Dublin, O'Donnell Lecture, 1962.
2 *In re Castioni* [1891] 1 QB 149.
3 *In re Meunier* [1894] 2 QB 415.

CHAPTER TWO

1 *In re Kaine*, 55 U.S. (14 How) 103-48.
2 *In re Ezeta*, 62F. 972 (N.D. California 1894).
3 *Ornelas v. Ruiz*, [1896] 161 U.S. 502.
4 James Lynchehaun Defense Committee, *An Irish American Victory over Great Britain*, Indianapolis, 1903.

CHAPTER THREE

1 Sir John Anderson to S.G. Tallents, 28 February 1923. Tallents papers, in private hands.
2 *R. v. Secretary of State for Home Affairs, ex parte O'Brien* [1923] AC.603.
3 *O'Boyle and Rodgers v. Attorney-General and General O'Duffy* [1929] 43 I.L.T.R. 33.
4 Parliament of Northern Ireland, *Parliamentary Debates: Official Report* (Hansard) *Senate*, Vol. 12 col. 453 (14 October 1930)
5 State Paper Office (SPO), Dublin, S 5340/7.
6 SPO S 2737.
7 SPO S 6419A.
8 Bowman, John, *De Valera and the Ulster Question, 1917-73* Clarendon Press, Oxford, 1982, p.198.

CHAPTER FOUR

1 Parliament of the United Kingdom, *Parliamentary Debates: Official Report* (Hansard) *House of Lords* Vol 134, cols. 927-8 and 939 (7 February 1945).
2 O'Higgins, Paul, *Irish Extradition Law and Practice*, British Yearbook of International Law, No. 54, 1958, pp.302-3.

3 *The State (Duggan) v. Tapley* [1952] Irish Reports 62.

4 Dáil Éireann, *Parliamentary Debates* Vol. 144, col. 1285 (4 March 1954).

5 Parliament of Northern Ireland, *Parliamentary Debates: Official Report* (Hansard) *House of Commons*, Vol. 51 cols. 69-70 (14 March 1962).

6 Dáil Éireann, *Parliamentary Debates*, Vol. 153 cols. 1336-1350 (30 November 1955).

7 *Ibid*, Vol. 194, cols 1212-3 (4 April 1962).

8 *The State (Quinn) v. Ryan* [1964] 98 *Irish Law Times and Solicitors Journal* 394.

9 Dáil Éireann, *Parliamentary Debates*, Vol. 207, cols. 79-138 (29 January 1964).

10 *Ibid*, Vol. 215, cols. 1879-1903 (20 May 1965).

CHAPTER FIVE

1 *The State (Magee) v. O'Rourke* [1971] Irish Reports 205-216.

2 *Bourke v. the Attorney-General* [1972] Irish Reports 36-68.

3 Quoted in *Violence and Civil Disturbances in Northern Ireland in 1969, Report of the Tribunal of Inquiry* (Scarman Report), Cmd. 566, HMSO, Belfast 1972. Vol. 2, Appendix A (vii).

4 *Irish Press*, 5 December 1973.

5 *Bartholomew Burns v. the Attorney-General*, unreported, 4 February 1974.

6 *Irish Press*, 21 December 1974.

CHAPTER SIX

1 *Report of the Law Enforcement Commission*, Prl. 3832, Dublin: The Stationery Office, 1974.

2 *R. v. Governor of Brixton Prison ex parte Kolczynski* [1955] 1 Q.B. 540.

3 *R. v. Governor of Brixton Prison ex parte Schtraks* [1964] A.C. 556.

4 *Matter of Doherty by the government of the United Kingdom*, 599 F. Supp. 270 (SDNY 1984).

5 *Irish Press*, 14 April 1970.

6 *R. v. Governor of Brixton Prison ex parte Keane* [1971] 1 A11. E.R. 1163.

7 *R. v. Governor Winson Green Prison ex parte Littlejohn* [1975] I. Weekly Law Reports 893.

8 *Re Taylor*, 5 N.I.M.R. 1.

9 Dáil Éireann, *Parliamentary Debates*, Vol. 292, cols. 6-8 (31 August 1976).

10 *Ibid.*, Vol. 285, col. 1676 (20 November 1975).

11 *Ibid.*, Vol. 279, col. 1228 (9 April 1975).

12 *Ireland v. United Kingdom of Great Britain and Northern Ireland* Judgement of the European Court of Human Rights, 18 January 1978.

13 *Report of the Committee of Inquiry into Police Interrogation Procedures in Northern Ireland* (Bennett Report) Cmnd. 7497, London HMSO; 1979.

CHAPTER SEVEN
1 *Karadzole v. Artukovic*, 247 F. 2d 198 (9th Circuit 1957) and *United States ex rel. Karadzole v. Artukovic*, 170 F. Supp. 383 (S.D.Cal. 1959).
2 *Ramos v. Diaz*, 179 F. Supp. 459 (S.D.Fla. 1959).
3 *In re McMullen*, Magis. No. 3 - 78 - 1099 (N.D. Cal. May 11, 1979).
4 *Abu Eian v. Wilkes*, 641 F. 2d 504 (7 Cir. 1981).
5 *In re Mackin*, 80 Cr.Misc. 1 (S.D.N.Y. 13 Aug. 1981), and *In re Matter of Mackin*, 668 F. 2d 122 (2 Cir. 1981).
6 *Quinn v. Robinson*, No C-82-6688 PPA (N.D.Cal. Oct. 3, 1983).

CHAPTER EIGHT
1 *Hanlon v. Fleming*, 5 October 1981, unreported.
2 *McGlinchey v. Wren*, 3 *Irish Law Reports Monthly* 169.
3 *Irish Press*, 9 December 1982.
4 *McMahon v. Governor of Mountjoy Prison and David Leahy*, 26 June 1984, unreported.
5 *Shannon v. Fanning*, 31 July 1984, unreported.

CHAPTER NINE
1 *Irish Press*, 25-27 December 1984.
2 *Irish Times*, 6 September 1984.
3 *Irish Independent*, 21 March 1985.
4 *Sunday Press*, 13 January 1985; *Irish Times*, 14 January 1985.
5 *Shannon v. Ireland and the Attorney-General*, High Court, 11 May 1984, unreported.
6 *Shannon v. Ireland and the Attorney-General*, Supreme Court, 16 November 1984, unreported.
7 *Matter of Doherty by the Government of the United Kingdom*, 599 F. Supp. 270. (S.D.N.Y. 1984).
8 *Irish Times*, 6 February 1985.
9 *Quinn v. Wren*, 28 February 1985.
10 The Supreme Court overturned this decision in July 1985. Mr Justice Walsh, for the court, held that there was not sufficient evidence to indicate that the robbery was carried out on behalf of the IRA. He did not comment on the question of whether IRA-linked offences could any longer be regarded as political. *Maguire v. Keane* unreported 31 July 1985.

CONCLUSION
1 *Sunday Press*, 13 January 1985.
2 *Ireland v. the United Kingdom of Great Britain and Northern Ireland*; judgement of the European Court of Human Rights, 18 January 1978.

3 Amnesty International, *Report of an Amnesty International Mission to Northern Ireland* (28 November — 6 December 1977), London, June 1978.
4 *Report of the Committee of Inquiry into Police Interrogation Procedures in Northern Ireland* (Bennett Report), Cmnd. 7497, London: HMSO 1979.
5 New Ireland Forum, *Report*, Dublin: The Stationery Office, May 1984.
6 *Irish Times*, 4 April and 6 June 1984.
7 *Irish Times* (Belfast), 10 August 1984.
8 *Irish Times*, 17 September 1984.

Acknowledgements

I could not have written this book without the generous help of a number of people and most notably a number of lawyers — in the Republic of Ireland, the North of Ireland and in the United States — who gave generously of their time and experience to guide me through the complexities of extradition law. I would like to thank all those who helped me, while pointing out that the responsibility for any errors and for opinions expressed is my own. Those who gave me special help in the legal field were (in the Republic): Seán MacBride SC, Patrick McEntee SC, Seamus Sorahan SC, Anthony Sammon BL, Eamon Coffey BL, Kader Asmal, Dean of Arts TCD, Gregg O'Neill BCL, Anne Rowland BCL; (in the United States) Mary Pike, Steve Somerstein and Paul O'Dwyer; (in the North of Ireland) P.J. McGrory Ll.B., Joe Rice Ll.B. and Patrick Fahy Ll.B. Dr Seán Cronin gave me valuable information about Napper Tandy and about the Fenians in the United States, Uinseann MacEoin gave me details of the Harry White case and Professor James Carney kindly allowed me to consult the manuscript of his book on James Lynchehaun. I am also grateful to Ms MacQuinn of the Supreme Court office for helping me obtain copies of Supreme Court judgements and to Seán Whelan of the Department of Foreign Affairs for information about extradition treaties. I would also like to thank Noirín Green and the staff of the *Irish Press* library for their generous assistance. Rita Byrne did her usual splendid job of typing an untidy manuscript and my wife Orla gave me invaluable help with research as well as having to live with the writing process.

A Message To The Irish People
Sean MacBride

Sean MacBride's views and proposals on: The Slave Mentality; Unemployment; The Trilateral Commission; The Atlantic Council; Neutrality; The Royal Irish Academy; Partition; Inland Waterways; Disarmament; Hunger Strikes; Afforestation.

Bobby Sands and the Tragedy of Northern Ireland
John M. Feehan

Bobby Sands captured the imagination of the world when, despite predictions, he was elected a Member of Parliament to the British House of Commons while still on hunger-strike in the Northern Ireland concentration camp of Long Kesh.

— When he later died after sixty-six gruelling days of hunger he commanded more television, radio and newspaper coverage than the papal visits or royal weddings.

— What was the secret of this young man who set himself against the might of an empire and who became a microcosm) of the whole Northern question and a moral catalyst for the Southern Irish conscience?

— In calm, restrained language John M. Feehan records the life of Bobby Sands with whom he had little sympathy at the beginning — though this was to change. At the same time he gives us an illuminating and crystal-clear account of the terrifying statelet of Northern Ireland today and of the fierce guerrilla warfare that is rapidly turning Northern Ireland into Britain's Vietnam.

The Informers

A Chilling Account of the Supergrasses
in Northern Ireland

Andrew Boyd

' . . . the latest in a long line of discredited legal strategies, which included internment and the Castlereagh interrogation centres.'
Association of Socialist Lawyers

'. . . a travesty of both legal and natural justice.'
Martin Flannery, MP

'. . . the courts themselves are on trial.'
The Times, 13 September 1983

'. . . uncorroborated evidence, unsafe evidence, and dangerous evidence was being relied upon.'
Gene Turner from the US Congress

'The practice of giving immunity to the most terrible terrorists and then using their uncorroborated evidence to put someone else in prison is bound to bring the law, those who make the law, and those who enforce the law into total disrepute.'
Councillor Sam Wilson, DUP

'Most of the checks for people to prove their innocence have been done away with. I'm very concerned with the situation.'
Noël Saint-Pierre of the Québec Jurists Association

With one hand extended in what appears to be gestures of reform and conciliation and the other encased in the mailed gauntlet of repression the British have blundered through another fifteen years of political violence. Now they have turned to the use of informers.

Northern Ireland: Who is to Blame?

Andrew Boyd

– Why did Westminster remain silent while the Unionists operated a permanent machine of dictatorship under the shadow of the British Constitution?

– Why have the Southern governments let Britain hand over the lives and liberties of the minority to the Orange Institution?

– Is the weakness of Labour in the North due to the fact that neither the NILP nor the ICTU have ever had any policies that would distinguish them from the Unionists?

– What help have Fianna Fáil, Fine Gael and the Labour Party offered to the minority north of the border?

Northern Ireland: Who is to Blame? examines the events and political attitudes and ideologies in both islands that have brought Northern Ireland to its present state of dangerous instability.

Have the Trade Unions Failed the North?

Andrew Boyd

– Is the fundamental and universal principle of trade unions – *an injury to one is an injury to all* – completely ignored by the unions in Ireland?

– What has been the record of the ICTU in dealing with unemployment, low wages, poverty, civil rights and, above all, the problem of sectarian discrimination in employment?

– How have the unions dealt with the social and political problems of the six counties?

– Do the trade unions resent facts about discrimination in the North being published?

– Why has the trade union movement conformed willingly to the wishes of the government?

– Do the grants that unions receive undermine the independence of the trade union movement?

– What contribution has the ICTU made towards making Northern Ireland more tolerant and non-sectarian?

Fine Gael: British or Irish?

Kevin Boland

— Is the excessive zeal in the repression of its enemies one of the main factors inhibiting real public confidence in Fine Gael of the order required for an overall majority?

— Is the complete ruthlessness in the suppression of Republicans still a fundamental part of the party's policy?

— Is the present day party dedicated to getting the people to proclaim in their Constitution that the claim to national unity is not based on the principles of democracy and justice but is a mere aspiration rightfully subject to the armed veto of a dissident minority — even when we are told that force achieves nothing?

— Do Fine Gael consider themselves enlightened realists against thick-headed diehards, the upholders of law and order against rebels and subversives, of peace against violence?

Operation Brogue

A Study of the Vilification of Charles J. Haughey Code-named Operation Brogue by the British Secret Service

John M. Feehan

— This book examines some recent events in the political life of Charles J. Haughey and questions the role played by the British Secret Service in a campaign of denigration against him believed to have been given the code-name Operation Brogue.

— It looks at the reasons why the British would want to destroy Mr Haughey in the context of their military needs to extend their strategic influence throughout the Republic.

— It explores the danger posed to these British strategic interests by Mr Haughey and his unwillingness to allow the Republic to be exploited by outside interests or to be made subservient to them.

— It outlines a number of standard techniques used by the British to mould people of standing and influence to their way of thinking.

— It considers how far the media gave a one-sided account of events to the detriment of Mr Haughey and suggests a lot of pertinent questions which they should have asked but did not.

— Finally it looks at Mr Haughey's role in the future and examines the question as to whether he is the person to lead the country out of its present state of near despair.

Skylark Sing Your Lonely Song
An anthology of the writings of Bobby Sands
Introduced by Ulick O'Connor

This book paints a self-portrait of a remarkable man. Bobby Sands spent no less than nine of his short life of twenty-seven years in jail — and yet this book shows how well he could write. His 'Trilogy' has echoes of Wilde's *Ballad of Reading Gaol*; essays like 'I once had a Life' and 'I Fought a Monster Today' expound his political attitude and at the same time conjure up the day-by-day sufferings of Bobby Sands and his comrades in the H-Blocks — the bad food, the body-searches and the continual harassment. Written on toilet paper and scraps of paper with a biro refill and hidden inside Sands' own body, these writings mirror the struggle that won him a tragic fame throughout the world. He discusses the attitude of Irish politicians and the Catholic Church to the sacrifice being enacted by himself and his comrades. Most poignant of all, however, is 'The Lark', a beautiful parable of Sands' own long years of captivity that says 'I too have seen the outside of the cage.'

This book will appeal to the great mass of readers, whether they are interested in politics or not. Bobby Sands' defiant spirit shines through. A book to be enjoyed by anyone who admires courage, wit and eloquence in the face of Death itself.

Bobby Sands was twenty-seven years old when he died, on the sixty-sixth day of his hunger strike, on 5 May 1981. By the time of his death he was world famous for having embarrassed the British establishment by being elected as M.P. to the British Parliament for Fermanagh/South Tyrone and having defiantly withstood political and moral pressure to abandon his hunger-strike.